HELPING CHILDREN TO
MANAGE STRESS

Also part of the Helping Children to Build Wellbeing and Resilience series

Helping Children to Manage Anger
Photocopiable Activity Booklet to Support Wellbeing and Resilience
Deborah M. Plummer
Illustrated by Alice Harper
ISBN 978 1 78775 863 6
eISBN 978 1 78775 864 3

Helping Children to Manage Transitions
Photocopiable Activity Booklet to Support Wellbeing and Resilience
Deborah M. Plummer
Illustrated by Alice Harper
ISBN 978 1 78775 861 2
eISBN 978 1 78775 862 9

Using Imagination, Mindful Play and Creative Thinking to Support Wellbeing and Resilience in Children
Deborah M. Plummer
Illustrated by Alice Harper
eISBN 978 1 78775 867 4

Helping Children to Manage Friendships
Photocopiable Activity Booklet to Support Wellbeing and Resilience
Deborah M. Plummer
Illustrated by Alice Harper
ISBN 978 1 78775 868 1
eISBN 978 1 78775 869 8

Helping Children to Build Communication Skills
Photocopiable Activity Booklet to Support Wellbeing and Resilience
Deborah M. Plummer
Illustrated by Alice Harper
ISBN 978 1 78775 870 4
eISBN 978 1 78775 871 1

Helping Children to Build Self-Confidence
Photocopiable Activity Booklet to Support Wellbeing and Resilience
Deborah M. Plummer
Illustrated by Alice Harper
ISBN 978 1 78775 872 8
eISBN 978 1 78775 873 5

Helping Children *to* Manage Stress

Photocopiable Activity Booklet to Support
Wellbeing and Resilience

Deborah M. Plummer

Illustrations by Alice Harper

Jessica Kingsley Publishers
London and Philadelphia

First published in Great Britain in 2022 by Jessica Kingsley Publishers
An imprint of Hodder & Stoughton Ltd
An Hachette Company

Some material was first published in *Using Interactive Imagework with Children* [1998], *Self-Esteem Games for Children* [2006], *Helping Children to Build Self-Esteem* [2007], *Helping Children to Cope with Change, Stress and Anxiety* [2008], *Anger Management Games for Children* [2008], *Social Skills Games for Children* [2008], and *Focusing and Calming Games for Children* [2012]. This edition first published in Great Britain in 2022 by Jessica Kingsley Publishers.

1

A CIP catalogue record for this title is available from the British Library and the Library of Congress

ISBN 978 1 78775 865 0
eISBN 978 1 78775 866 7

Printed and bound in Great Britain by Bell & Bain Limited

Jessica Kingsley Publishers' policy is to use papers that are natural, renewable and recyclable products and made from wood grown in sustainable forests. The logging and manufacturing processes are expected to conform to the environmental regulations of the country of origin.

Jessica Kingsley Publishers
Carmelite House
50 Victoria Embankment
London EC4Y 0DZ

www.jkp.com

Contents

Acknowledgements

I have collected or devised the games and activities in this series of books over a 30-year period of working first as a speech and language therapist with children and adults, and then as a lecturer and workshop facilitator. Some were contributed by children during their participation in therapy groups or by teachers and therapists during workshops and discussions. Thank you!

The suggestions for adaptations and the expansion activities have arisen from my experiences of running children's groups. Many of them combine elements of ImageWork (Dr Dina Glouberman), Personal Construct Theory (see, for example, Peggy Dalton and Gavin Dunnett) and Solution-Focused Brief Therapy (Insoo Kim Berg and Steve de Shazer). My thanks therefore go to my teachers and mentors in these fields.

I have also found the following books helpful:

- Arnold, A. (1976) *The World Book of Children's Games*. London: Pan Books Ltd.
- Beswick, C. (2003) *The Little Book of Parachute Play*. London: Featherstone Education Ltd.
- Brandes, D. and Phillips, H. (1979) *Gamesters' Handbook: 140 Games for Teachers and Group Leaders*. London: Hutchinson.
- Dunn, O. (1978) *Let's Play Asian Children's Games*. Macmillan Southeast Asia in association with the Asian Cultural Centre for UNESCO.
- Liebmann, M. (2004) *Art Therapy for Groups: A Handbook of Themes and Exercises* (2nd edition). London and New York: Routledge.
- Masheder, M. (1989) *Let's Play Together*. London: Green Print.
- Neelands, J. (1990) *Structuring Drama Work: A Handbook of Available Forms in Theatre and Drama*. Cambridge: Cambridge University Press.

Note: There are many different non-competitive 'mini' games that can be used for choosing groups, coordinators (leaders) and order of play where appropriate. I have listed several options in the accompanying eBook Using Imagination, Mindful Play and Creative Thinking to Support Wellbeing and Resilience in Children. *I suggest that the format is varied between sessions so that children can experiment with different ways of doing this. The choosing then becomes part of the personal learning.*

The following icons are used throughout to indicate the three elements of the IMPACT approach:

Imagination

Mindful Play

Creative Thinking

Introduction

This book is one of a series based on the use of Imagination (I), Mindful Play (MP) and Creative Thinking (CT) to enhance social, psychological and emotional wellbeing and resilience in children. IMPACT activities and strategies encourage children to build life skills through carefully structured and supportive play experiences. Emphasis is given to the important role played by adult facilitators in creating a safe space in which children can share and explore feelings and difficulties and experiment with different ways of thinking and 'being'. This approach is explained in the accompanying eBook *Using Imagination, Mindful Play and Creative Thinking to Support Wellbeing and Resilience in Children*, which also contains many further ideas for games and activities and examples of how the IMPACT approach can enhance daily interactions with children.

Please remember, if you are a parent or carer and you are concerned about ongoing and persistently high levels of anxiety or aggressive behaviour, or persistently low mood in your child, it is always best to seek further support via your child's school or your child's doctor. This book is not intended as a substitute for the professional help that may be needed when children are experiencing clinically recognized difficulties such as chronic school phobia, severe social anxiety or childhood depression.

USING THIS BOOK

The games and activities in this book help children to:

- identify some of their worries
- build skills and strategies that will help them to recognize normal signs of stress and to respond to these appropriately
- explore the possible benefits and enjoyment of positive stress.

The IMPACT approach emphasizes eight *foundation elements* for wellbeing (see the accompanying eBook *Using Imagination, Mindful Play and Creative Thinking to Support Wellbeing and Resilience in Children*). Although all eight of these elements are closely interconnected, the focus for the games and activities in this book centres on three of the elements that are particularly relevant when thinking about managing mild to moderate amounts of stress: *self-awareness*, *self-acceptance* and *self-reliance*. Here is a reminder of what these three foundation elements encapsulate:

Self-awareness

Self-awareness is the cornerstone of realistic self-evaluation. It involves:

- developing the ability to be focused in the here and now rather than being absorbed in unhelpful thoughts about the past or future – this includes awareness and identification of feelings as they arise
- developing the ability to switch attention appropriately from external events to internal thoughts and feelings and vice versa
- understanding that emotional, mental and physical changes are a natural part of life
- being aware of the normality of a range of feelings and how these link to thoughts and behaviour.

The IMPACT approach offers a forum in which feelings are acknowledged, valued and openly discussed in a non-judgemental way. The games and activities help children to develop the ability to switch attention effectively between internal and external stimuli, cope more effectively with distractions, make informed choices about how and when to focus their attention, monitor their internal 'self-talk' and build effective strategies for self-calming.

Self-acceptance

Recognizing personal strengths and achievements and being able to accept sincere praise and compliments are important aspects of self-acceptance. This element also involves:

- recognizing what can't be changed
- recognizing areas of personal difficulty that may require the development or refining of skills

- understanding the difference between experimenting and failing (young children are often not aware that older children and adults make 'mis-takes' in their experimenting too, and that this can be a very productive way of learning)
- developing and maintaining positive body awareness.

IMPACT games, activities and strategies help children to recognize and celebrate their strengths, tolerate mild frustration and develop the capacity to recognize and accept supportive feedback from others. They aim to help children to recognize times when they are able to focus and concentrate successfully and to acknowledge times when this might be difficult, perhaps because of distracting internal thoughts and feelings (especially when these are self-limiting thoughts, such as 'I can't do this') or external circumstances (such as a noisy environment over which they have no control). Activities also aim to enhance positive body awareness so that children can, for example, let go of unwanted tension or focus on calm breathing, and learn to use body awareness to further develop their capacity for being mindful.

Self-reliance

This element involves:

- developing physical, mental and emotional self-care skills
- building a measure of independence and self-motivation
- reducing reliance on other people's opinions and evaluations
- expanding awareness of current strengths and developing the ability to realistically assess personal progress
- learning to set realistic yet challenging goals or accept the need to modify a goal.

When children start to develop a degree of self-reliance they are more able to enjoy the exciting and fun things in life and are more ready to cope with things that are challenging or difficult. Of course, the capacity for self-reliance is acquired very gradually in childhood, but each step can be a tremendous boost to self-esteem and general wellbeing, especially if it is noted and celebrated. Children's physical achievements, such as being able to dress themselves or ride a bike, are often acknowledged and celebrated, but there are other areas of self-reliance that may be missed by the child and by adults as well. These small triumphs of *emotional* self-care can be a powerful force for increased motivation, independent thinking, self-efficacy and emotional resilience, and we can help by being on the look-out for them and encouraging them just as much as the physical signs of self-reliance.

The IMPACT approach provides opportunities for supporting children in building self-reliance by actively promoting feelings of being in control, and by helping children in their growing abilities to anticipate and predict what might happen next, both as a consequence of their own behaviour and of other people's behaviour. This is an important factor in successfully managing potentially stressful events.

IMPACT strategies and activities also encourage and support children in forming realistic and manageable goals.

Facilitator involvement

All the games and activities in this series of books offer opportunities for facilitators to take an active part. Our participation reflects the nature of extended communities and gives us an opportunity to have fun alongside the children. Throughout the games in this book, the term 'game coordinator' therefore refers to either adult or child participants, as appropriate for the level and stage of each group.

Activities

The first section of games and activities, 'IMPACT Essentials for Managing Stress' (section II), introduces children to the central features of the IMPACT approach – using imagery, being mindful and thinking creatively. There are also activities for group 'gelling' and for exploring relevant concepts such as self-respect and respect for others. Each book in this series has a different set of IMPACT essentials. With a slight change of emphasis, you will be able to use any of these to supplement your sessions if needed.

The remaining sections are arranged in accordance with specific aspects of managing stress: 'Thinking and Feeling', 'Exploring Strategies', 'Self-Calming' and 'Wind Downs and Completions'.

You might also find it useful to add a selection of games and activities from *Helping Children to Manage Anger*, which is available in this series. This looks at how we might help children to handle strong (and therefore potentially stressful) emotions.

The creative potential for supporting skill development is one of the wonderful features of childhood games. I have given several suggestions for specific skills that might be learned or further developed during each game and its associated activities, but these are not exhaustive. You may want to add more to suit your own focus of work.

Ideas are also suggested for adaptations. (See also Chapter 12, 'Adapting Activities', in *Using Imagination, Mindful Play and Creative Thinking to Support Wellbeing and Resilience in Children*.) These illustrate some of the many ways in which a basic game can be simplified or made more complex to suit diverse developmental levels, strengths and learning differences.

Reflection and discussion

Another important aspect of all the games and activities is the opportunity they provide for children to expand their thinking skills. To aid this process, I have included suggestions for further reflection and discussion ('Talk about'). These include a mixture of possible prompt questions and suggestions for comments or explanations that can be useful when introducing or elaborating some of the ideas. (See Chapter 11, 'Mindful Communication', and Chapter 13, 'Mindful Praise and Appreciation', in *Using Imagination, Mindful Play and Creative Thinking to Support Wellbeing and Resilience in Children* for more ideas about facilitating discussions with children.) You may want to select just a couple of these or spread the discussion over several sessions.

These discussion topics also provide an opportunity for drawing links between different themes at later times. You could remind children of particular games or activities when this is relevant: 'Do you remember when we played that game of... What did you find out about focusing attention?' or 'How might the mindful breathing activity be useful to us in this situation?'

Expansion activities

Many of the main games or activities are followed by one or more expansion activities. These are an important part of the process too. They encourage children to recognize the benefits of a stepped approach to learning and to the process of change, understand how new skills can build on previous experiences, and understand how current skills can be strengthened.

Activity sheets

Some of the expansion activities have accompanying activity sheets that can also be adapted for discussion, these can be found in section VII. I have found that children particularly like to draw or write about their imaginary world. Their drawings and jottings might then be the starting point for wellbeing stories (see *Using Imagination, Mindful Play and Creative Thinking to Support Wellbeing and Resilience in Children* for ideas about how to create these stories). They can also be made into a personal 'Book of Wisdom' and perhaps act as reminders of some of the strategies that children might want to use again in the future.

Note: Please keep in mind that IMPACT activity sheets are offered as supplementary material to expand and reinforce each child's learning experiences. They are not intended as stand-alone alternatives to the mindful play and supportive discussions that are central to the IMPACT approach.

Exploring Stress

'Stress' is a word we are all very familiar with. In everyday language it is generally used to indicate the negative effects of life pressures: 'I feel stressed out', 'I'm so stressed, I can't think straight', 'My migraines are getting more frequent because of the stress I'm under'. In fact, a certain amount of stress is useful and necessary. Stress helps us to adapt to change. It is one of the factors that motivate us to achieve. It can be a stimulus for action and is an important element for success in many areas of performance such as music, dance and sport. Moderate or short-term amounts of stress can enhance memory and learning (although prolonged stress is known to reduce memory capacity and the ability to learn). Coping successfully with a stressful but potentially enjoyable situation such as learning to swim or to climb trees can be a real boost to a child's self-esteem, and moderate amounts of stress are a natural part of growing up. However, long-term stress or repeated bouts of stress are much more likely to be detrimental to wellbeing.

Connie is 10 years old. Her father has a new job in another part of the country and has been commuting to and from home at weekends for the last eight months. The family have now made arrangements to move so that they can spend more time together. Connie's parents have always spoken about the move in very positive terms, and in order not to disrupt their daughter's last year at primary school, the move will take place during the summer holidays.

Despite her parents' support and positive attitude, Connie is showing signs of increasing anxiety. Small obstacles now appear to her to be major problems. She is not sleeping well, often waking two or three times in the night having had a 'bad' dream. She appears tired and listless at school and has reverted to some comfort behaviours from her earlier childhood, including wanting to have her bedroom light left on at night. She insists on phoning her father every day while he is at work and is terrified that he will have an accident on his commute home at weekends. She worries that her mother will forget to pick her up from school, that her younger brother will get lost in the shops, that she won't have the right kit for her lessons at her new school, and that she will never make any new friends. Her list of worries is growing each day.

Connie may be naturally sensitive to change and prone to anxiety – her physiological system pre-programmed to be in a heightened state of alertness when under stress, constantly on the look-out for anything that could be seen as threatening or dangerous. This hyper-alertness is physically and emotionally exhausting, and anyone in this state will naturally crave to re-establish a sense of normality and control in their lives. Unfortunately, the ways in which we do this, either consciously or unconsciously, can sometimes be detrimental to our wellbeing.

EMOTION REGULATION

The rapid and relatively recent growth in the field of neurosciences has provided important insights into the connections between physiological development, early life experiences and what happens when we are under stress. This helps us to understand the best mechanisms for helping children to cope as they grow and change, and to help them to develop strategies that are appropriate and adaptable for all stages of life.

We know, for example, that one of the primary developmental tasks in the emotional life of a young child is to establish an effective emotion-regulation system: the ability to self-regulate and self-calm so that they are not constantly overwhelmed with difficult emotions. Two areas of the brain are particularly important in the development of this self-regulatory capacity: the amygdala and the pre-frontal cortex.

The *amygdala*, a small almond-shaped area of interconnected structures located on each side of the brain within the temporal lobes, plays a major part in how we experience emotions and is responsible for detecting threat and initiating the stress response (fight, flight or freeze) quickly and efficiently, without the need for thoughtful analysis of the situation.[1] The amygdala sends information to the hypothalamus (which is concerned with regulating various systems within the body, including the release of stress hormones). The amygdala has been shown to be involved in the laying down of immediate and long-lasting emotional memories associated with perceived threat. For

1   See the accompanying eBook *Using Imagination, Mindful Play and Creative Thinking to Support Wellbeing and Resilience in Children* for an outline of how meditation is thought to affect the amygdala.

example, when a person or object is associated (even by chance) with a traumatic event, the amygdala will produce such a strong neuronal response that a future encounter with that same person or object will trigger the stress response, regardless of whether or not any actual threat is present.[2]

The amygdala's rapid response to perceived threat can be regulated by other areas of the brain, for example the pre-frontal cortex, which deals with feelings and social interactions.

The *pre-frontal cortex*, as its name suggests, constitutes the front part of the frontal lobes. This area of the brain is most vulnerable to outside influences during its critical period of development in the first four years of life. Such influences include the ability of primary carers to tune into their child's feelings and provide the comfort and touch that allows the emotion-regulation system to develop and to function effectively. When the system is working well, impulsive reactions to a perceived threat can be inhibited or regulated via the 'thinking' processes carried out at this higher level, thereby preventing us from being overwhelmed, for example, by inappropriate fear or anxiety.

All children experience some stress in their lives without this producing strong adverse effects, but every child will be different in the amount of stress that they can deal with successfully and in how they perceive stressful situations in the first place. What one child sees as exciting and stimulating, another may see as completely terrifying.

Levels of resilience to stress will partly depend on a child's ability to moderate stress and on their coping strategies. These, in turn, will be influenced by their developmental stage, personal temperament, emotional maturity, environment, social support and past experiences. It is a combination of these internal and external resources that lead to the most effective physiological and psychological reactions to stress.

Research indicates three major ways in which stress can be psychologically mediated: seeing the stressor as a challenge rather than a threat, having a sense of being able to control a stressful circumstance, and having healthy self-esteem. Coping strategies might then be focused on dealing directly with the problem in some way (avoiding/walking away from a situation, taking physical exercise, talking it over with a good friend) or might involve changing the way we think about the problem ('This is quite exciting'), or learning to tolerate and accept it ('This is stressful but I can manage my stress levels well'). Coping techniques tend to be situation-specific, and what works for one stressor may not work for another.

---

2   Nunn, K., Hanstock, T. and Lask, B. (2008) *Who's Who of the Brain*. London and Philadelphia, PA: Jessica Kingsley Publishers.

SOME COMMON STRESSORS FOR CHILDREN

One of the biggest stressors for any child is the loss of (or fear of losing) a secure attachment. The link between a primary carer and child attachment patterns and a child's later ability to regulate their emotions has been the focus for much research. Attachment is thought to be the most important source of a child's security, self-esteem, self-control and social skills (see the accompanying eBook *Using Imagination, Mindful Play and Creative Thinking to Support Wellbeing and Resilience in Children*).

Some other common stressors for children include:

- speech, language and communication disorders and delay
- times of transition, including starting and changing school
- school pressures, including exams
- unrealistic pressure for consistently high standards of behaviour and conformity to rules
- bullying, teasing, difficulty in making friends, ending friendships, making new friends, feeling 'different' from peers
- illness or physical disability
- persistent under-stimulation (boredom)
- getting lost or fear of being lost in an unfamiliar place.

Often several stressors can interconnect. For example, when a child associates being loved and approved of with being 'good' or 'obedient' or achieving at school, then the type of stress that all children experience at times of change or times of assessment can be greatly magnified.

THE STRESS RESPONSE

There are some normal reactions that occur when we are faced with a stressful situation. These reactions prepare the body for 'fight or flight'. We each tend to develop individual patterns of stress reaction, with some of the fight or flight responses being more prominent than others. Specific stressful conditions and the ways in which we appraise these conditions can result in different emotional and physiological responses. Common signs include the following:

- Muscles tense for action, which can result in aches and pains or feeling 'shaky'.

- The heart pumps harder to get the blood where it is most needed in preparation for greater muscular effort. This may feel like palpitations and may also result in an increase in blood pressure.
- There is therefore less blood elsewhere, and so the skin often goes pale and the movements of the stomach slow down or stop (the cause of a sudden 'sinking feeling' in the stomach).
- The salivary glands dry up, resulting in a dry mouth or throat.
- Breathing may become faster because the lungs must take in more oxygen more rapidly and also get rid of carbon dioxide.
- The pupils of the eyes get bigger to let in more light and so increase sensitivity to incoming stimuli.
- The stress hormones, primarily adrenaline, are secreted to keep this stress reaction going.

If the reaction is completed and the 'danger' is dealt with, then the body can relax again. These are all very useful responses to actual threat or danger and the body usually returns to its normal level of functioning fairly quickly after the stressful event is over. Unfortunately, we often produce the fight or flight reaction in situations that don't actually need a physical response. These things may happen when children are concerned about a test, a potentially difficult conversation, being in the school play or being late for a school trip. What is even more of a problem is that negative self-talk tends to prolong the stress response. If children tell themselves that they can't cope, then their body will continue to stay ready for action. Unwanted stress reactions can also occur when the original stressful situation is no longer there, but the child has not done anything to ease the stress response.

THE EFFECTS OF STRESS

When stress is excessive or continuous over a long period of time, even at relatively low levels, we will experience a 'toxic' build-up of stress hormones such as cortisol, which is released by the adrenal glands. Under normal circumstances, cortisol is useful – it plays an important part in helping us to regulate our emotions and the rhythms of our days. For example, levels of cortisol usually rise first thing in the morning to help give us energy and then dip later in the afternoon. Cortisol also has an important role in raising blood glucose levels and in breaking down fat and other proteins to provide extra energy for the fight or flight reaction. However, persistently high levels of cortisol can affect our memory capacity and will dampen our immune system (hence the common phenomenon of people falling ill when they go on holiday after a prolonged stressful period at work). This, coupled with a fall in levels of dopamine and serotonin (the feel-good hormones) in the pre-frontal cortex, can cause us to feel 'overwhelmed, fearful, and miserable, colouring our thoughts, feelings, and perceptions with a sense of threat or dread as if everything we need to do is far too hard'.[3]

THINKING, FEELING, DOING

With increasing maturity, a child's thought processes and the ways in which they appraise situations will also start to play a bigger part in how they interpret and regulate their emotions. When they experience a state of arousal, such as when they are anxious, they will check out what is going on around them in order to find an explanation and will also draw on past events and 'emotion memories'. Although the links that they make may be largely subconscious, these can still inform their present reactions. In this way, out of control experiences of feeling anxious in the past may, for instance, intensify current physiological arousal, which, in turn, confirms the child's appraisal of the situation and intensifies the experience of the emotion.

Images also play an important role in this process. If I tell myself to increase my heart rate or to sweat, I'm not likely to notice much response! But if I imagine a frightening experience vividly enough, my body will respond as if it is actually happening.

The influence of past experiences and the developing capacity to appraise situations as potentially threatening or stressful, combined with fluctuations in biochemical levels and the complex interactions between the pre-frontal cortex and the amygdala, conspire to make emotion regulation a real challenge for all of us. It is hardly surprising that children find this a tricky developmental task. Fortunately, there is much that can be done to help. The brain is remarkable in its capacity to adapt and respond to new influences, particularly during early childhood, and there are many natural childhood activities that help to promote this process.

---

3   Sunderland, M. (2006) *The Science of Parenting*. London: Dorling Kindersley, p.87. [There is now a second edition of this book, published in 2016.]

A MINDFUL PLAY PERSPECTIVE

The IMPACT approach to managing stress is based on mindful, creative, child-centred interactions. It reflects the view that children benefit from being active participants in developing and maintaining their own wellbeing, and that they also benefit from the mindful care of adults who will support them and help them to build resilience for future challenges. In order to get a feel for some of the games and activities in this book and how these relate to a child's experience of stress, I believe that it is helpful to start from our own perspectives.

How do we, as adults, deal with different types of stress in our own lives? How do we already support the children in our care as they negotiate stressful times? How can we maximize this support? Experiencing the following activities from an adult perspective will also undoubtedly trigger some thoughts about how you can adapt these and other games and activities in this book. There are no right or wrong answers to any of these; they are simply ways of exploring the topic.

Begin by setting aside a short period of uninterrupted time when you will have the opportunity to carry out and to reflect on a single activity – 10–15 minutes is probably ample. I suggest that you only do one activity and then go back to doing other things. Please don't be tempted to do all the activities one after the other in a single sitting, even if you have the time. A period of reflection is always useful after an exploratory activity.

Exploratory activity 1.1. Identifying stressors
(See 'Expansion activity 4.1. Finding out a bit more'.)

Make a list of five situations that you find stressful and five situations that you think a particular child finds stressful. Note some of the similarities and differences.

Now make a list of five situations that you have found challenging but rewarding and five situations that you think this child might find stressful but ultimately enjoyable. Again, notice any similarities and differences.

The complexity of interactions between personal temperament, internal and external resources, past experiences and current circumstances means that a single method for helping children to manage stress is unlikely to be a viable option. The IMPACT approach addresses this challenge by using a number of different but closely connected activities and strategies that are outlined below. These encourage children to develop or enhance flexibility of thought and focused awareness and promote feelings of self-efficacy. This, in turn, helps children to build emotional resilience and self-esteem, leading to greater feelings of wellbeing.

Recognizing tension and relaxation

Our posture and breathing patterns, like words and gestures, can be seen as ways in which we express our thoughts. When we are stressed we often show it in the way we sit, stand and walk. Simply becoming more aware of this and gently focusing on different areas of the body can help us to release unwanted tension and calm our minds.

One of the many ways of successfully controlling the adverse signs of stress is through learning specific relaxation strategies. These can be taught to children in a fun way, to relieve physical tension, to help them to relax emotionally and mentally, and to help them to feel at ease with themselves and with their feelings. Effective relaxation results in decreased metabolism and reduced blood pressure and breathing rate. Research has shown that it also produces the subjective feelings of calmness and stability, so this is a really vital skill for children to learn. As with any skill, regular practice will gradually lead to both short-term and long-term benefits. This book includes a variety of these exercises so that children can experiment with them and find which ones work best for their individual use.

It is also important to find an enjoyable relaxation method for yourself. Your own relaxed breathing and relaxed posture will provide a good model for children to follow and will, of course, produce long-lasting benefits in your own life.

Exploratory activity 1.2. Focusing (1)

Take a few moments to focus on different areas of your body and notice if your muscles are currently tensed or relaxed. Start with your feet and then allow the focus of your attention to gradually move along your body, ending with your neck, jaw and forehead. What other sensations do you notice? For example, are your feet warm, cold, tingling? Just notice what sensations are there without trying to change anything.

Sketch a body outline of yourself and jot down anything that you noticed.

Using imagery

(See Chapter 8, 'Imagination and Images', and Chapter 9, 'Image-Making', in the accompanying eBook *Using Imagination, Mindful Play and Creative Thinking to Support Wellbeing and Resilience in Children.*)

As noted earlier, if we imagine a stressful event vividly enough, the body will invariably react as if that event is actually happening. It makes sense to help children to realize how their thinking connects to how they feel physically, and to learn to harness their imagination in a positive way. Constructive use of the imagination is central to the IMPACT approach (see *Using Imagination, Mindful Play and Creative Thinking to Support Wellbeing and Resilience in Children*). Images have a remarkable capacity to sum up how we are feeling or how we view a situation. So, for example, if I ask you to allow an image to emerge into your thoughts that somehow represents how you are feeling physically right now, each reader will, of course, see, hear or sense something different (remember, images do not have to be visual). What image comes to mind for you?

I use this type of imagery on a regular basis, particularly while I am writing. One of the images that I have had in relation to tension was a baby dragon trying to stretch its wings – I had a pain in my shoulder that was aggravating me and I was finding it difficult to write. When I allowed myself a moment to step into being the baby dragon, I was keen to tell my 'self' (Deborah, sitting at the computer) that, although I was just a baby pain, I had the potential to cause aggravation to others by becoming more dragon-like unless I was soothed. I knew immediately that this was not just about me dealing with discomfort before it got worse (I can get very 'tetchy' when I am tired or in pain!). I realized that I should take a break. I made a note to myself to stay calm. I sensed the baby dragon settling into a more relaxed state.

The children I have worked with as a speech and language therapist have often come up with wonderfully vivid images for relaxation, such as 'eating jelly to relax my throat'. Creative imagery can provide a rich learning experience that goes beyond the teaching of skills as a way of coping 'after the event' and promotes feelings of personal fulfilment and self-respect. By encouraging children to listen to their thoughts and feelings and to note how their imagination can affect their body, we are teaching them to value themselves, and this will undoubtedly affect the way they interact with others and the way they deal with situations in the future.

Active play

Imaginative and creative play is known to reduce levels of stress chemicals, enabling children to deal more successfully with stressful situations. Gentle rough and tumble play and laughter are also known to have de-stressing effects, activating the brain's emotion-regulating centres and causing the release of opioids, the natural brain chemicals that induce feelings of pleasure and wellbeing.[4] Walking, cycling, playing sport or just playing outside in the fresh air can all be excellent ways for children to de-stress. There is an abundance of research on the beneficial effects to our health and wellbeing of being in green spaces. There is also increasing evidence that it is not just walking, running, cycling and playing in green spaces that is good for us. The sense of wellbeing is also enhanced by mindful attention to nature – focusing, observing, listening and sensing what is around us with all our attention, even if this is for relatively short periods of time.

Exploratory activity 1.3. Active play

Make a note of any hobbies that you engage with that you consider to be 'play' or 'playful'. What (for you) distinguishes playful activities from non-playful activities? If you can discuss this with one other person, note any differences and similarities in your responses.

Calm breathing

A calm breathing pattern is a vital factor in the management of stress. It's very easy to take our breathing for granted because it's an automatic activity and most people don't think about it on a conscious level. If you watch a baby or young child sleeping you will see the ideal breathing pattern – slow, full and regular. Their stomach will be rising and falling easily and smoothly. However, breathing patterns can change, sometimes over long periods of time. These changes might be brought about by health problems or occur as a reaction to prolonged stress or as a result of suppressed emotions ('Big children don't cry', for example). As well as these long-term changes, temporary changes will also occur at times of stress and as a reflection of different emotions. For example, anxiety often results in shallow, rapid breathing. Calm breathing will help children to see that they can have some control over their body when they are feeling nervous or stressed, and can help with potentially overwhelming emotions such as anger or fear.

---

4   Sunderland, M. (2006) *The Science of Parenting*. London: Dorling Kindersley. [There is now a second edition of this book, published in 2016.]

22

Exploratory activity 1.4. Breathing patterns

Check your own breathing pattern. Sit in a comfortable chair or stand in front of a full-length mirror. Place one hand lightly on your chest and the other hand on your stomach. Watch what happens as you take a full breath in and then release the air slowly.

Which hand moved the most? Did your shoulders rise? Did your stomach move in or out? Did your posture change in any way? If your breathing was relaxed you will have felt your stomach expanding as you breathed in and falling as you breathed out. This movement will have been very relaxed and gentle. There will have been only slight movement in your chest. Your shoulders will have hardly moved at all. Your posture will have remained balanced.

When we are physically tense or anxious we are more likely to use upper chest breathing. This type of breathing mainly involves the top half of the lungs.

If you push air out you will be tensing your intercostal muscles and your diaphragm on the out-breath. This type of forced expiration also involves muscles in the outer wall of the abdomen. These press upwards on to the bases of the lungs and force the lungs to become smaller so that air is forced out. All this extra tension increases the feelings of stress.

As you can see, there is a very close relationship between breathing and relaxation. If our breathing is tense, then our body cannot relax completely, and if our body is tense, then our breathing will not be as full and regular as it could be. Abdominal breathing helps us to feel calm and focused.

Focused breathing

Being aware of our breathing and training our mind to follow our breathing pattern (rather than being constantly preoccupied with other thoughts) for short periods each day can lead to increased feelings of general wellbeing and the ability to cope successfully with the stresses of daily life. There are several different games and activities in this book that will help children to focus their attention and to be mindful of their breathing. See, for example, '13. Mindful breathing' and '14. Combining breath control and imagery'.

Exploratory activity 1.5. Focusing (2)

Sit in a comfortable position, perhaps with your eyes closed so that you can focus completely on your breathing.

Start by simply being aware of your natural breathing pattern. If you are abdominal breathing already, then notice the rise and fall of your stomach. If you are upper chest breathing, then remember that the idea is to relax your stomach as much as possible.

When you have established a comfortable rhythm to your breathing, continue with the process for about five minutes. Your thoughts are bound to wander off onto other things. This is very natural. No matter how often this happens, just notice it, and then gently bring your mind back to focusing on the rise and fall of your stomach.

Take time to do this every day for a week, and notice any changes in how you feel when you are doing it.

Notice what happens if you take your attention to your breathing at various moments during each day. Notice what happens if you take time to establish awareness of abdominal breathing at times when you are feeling particularly stressed.

When you feel comfortable with five minutes of daily practice, begin to gradually lengthen the time that you sit quietly focusing on your breathing in this way. Aim to extend the time to 15 minutes a day.

A stepped approach

Altering personal ways of coping with stress is not always easy, particularly when focusing on and thinking about what we *don't* want has the unfortunate consequence of keeping it uppermost in our mind. In a way, it is like me saying to myself at the start of a presentation, 'Don't think about your itchy nose', or saying to a child 'Don't run in the corridor'. An alternative picture would be more useful: 'Focus on the audience', 'Walk quietly'. Imagine saying to yourself 'Don't get anxious!' before an important meeting. The image that you will have in your mind is likely to be of yourself being in an anxious state, and this may trigger the actual feelings of anxiety. However, if you explore your personal opposite of anxious and imagine this vividly enough, you will have a better sense of what that more desirable state entails, and it will be easier for you to see which elements you are already embracing and which elements you could enhance.

Exploratory activity 1.6. Pyramiding

This is based on an exercise from Personal Construct Theory.[5]

Think of a word or phrase that represents your personal view of the opposite of 'stressed'. Now think of a time when you are, or have been, in this positive mental, emotional and physical state. Let's say your personal opposite to stress is 'able to enjoy challenges'. At the top of a large sheet of paper write down four attributes that you possess that cause you to view yourself as 'able to enjoy challenges'. You could start off by thinking 'I know this because...'

Now take each of these four elements in turn and ask yourself *how* you know this. How do you demonstrate each attribute? How would other people know this about you? For example, if one of your words is 'flexible', think about how that can be broken down into smaller components. What does flexibility 'look' like? Do this for as many of your ideas as possible so that you are refining them into smaller and smaller constituents. Whenever you find yourself using a word or phrase that denotes a negative, such as 'not', 'never' or 'doesn't', look for a positive alternative. For example, if 'flexibility' includes 'doesn't get hung up on details' then you might change this to 'sees the bigger picture'. You could then further refine this by asking yourself 'what do I do, or what sort of language do I use, that conveys to others that I can see the bigger picture?'

Jo would like to be more creative in her approach to working with children. Her pyramid was based around a friend whom she considered to be a creative cook. She identified 'not worried about making mistakes' as one of the components of her view of creativity. When encouraged to turn this into a positive statement 'not worried about' became 'relaxed about' and 'able to learn from mis-takes'. She further refined 'mis-takes' into 'experiments' so that her opposite of worry became 'relaxed about experimenting and adapting'.

Looking at the smaller elements of a concept gives us an insight into how we or others

5   See, for example, Dalton, P. and Dunnett, G. (2005) *A Psychology for Living: Personal Construct Theory for Professionals and Clients* (2nd edition). Chichester: John Wiley & Sons Ltd.

view that concept, and being more specific about behaviour and feelings can open up avenues for appropriate support.

> Aisha's mother recognized that she frequently referred to Aisha as a 'shy' child. Reflecting on more specific behaviours helped her to think about possible ways to help: 'At the moment she is unsure of herself when she first arrives somewhere new. It takes her a while to build the confidence to talk to new people. It might help if we practised some things that she could say.'

Positive touch

One of the most natural reactions to stress is to give ourselves a gentle massage. Perhaps you have noticed yourself massaging your neck or your temple. This can help to relieve pain but can also be a self-calming mechanism. Massage is thought to help the body return to normal functioning after a stressful event, and we also know that levels of hormones such as oxytocin (the hormone known to aid the 'bonding' process after childbirth) and serotonin (the 'feel-good' hormone that helps us to relax) vary enormously according to how much positive physical contact children experience. The release of oxytocin triggered by positive touch such as being cuddled or given a gentle massage by a parent or carer contributes to feelings of safety and comfort and is associated with the regulation of cortisol (see *Using Imagination, Mindful Play and Creative Thinking to Support Wellbeing and Resilience in Children*).

In the context of IMPACT games and activities, any massage element is always given by children to other children and is only focused on the upper back, arms, hands and head. If you want to demonstrate a massage game you will need to borrow another adult for your massage partner – in my experience, you will never be short of volunteers for this! Each child should always ask their partner for their permission to give a massage before beginning, and it is okay for children to say 'no thank you'.

The final section of this book offers some simple self-calming strategies specifically for children. There are also activities throughout other sections that are suitable for adapting for individual use. For example, I have included a massage activity where children give each other a gentle back massage ('21. Circle massage'). This can easily be adapted to a self-calming massage – each child giving themselves a gentle pretend shampoo, for example, or massaging their own hands by imagining that their fingers are the legs and trunks of two young elephants giving each other a gentle mud bath!

Music

Although evidently not appropriate for use during a focus activity (see '11. Body focus'), it is well worth experimenting with music in activities when your aim is to extend children's awareness of different self-calming strategies (see, for example, '22. Musical drawing'). I have used gentle music as a lead-in to guided visualizations with children and also during the rest periods after a full relaxation session. Many of the children in our speech and language therapy groups asked for details of this music so that they could use it at home. We know, too, that even if we are unable to be outside, listening to pre-recorded sounds of nature can also have a calming effect. Children are unlikely to try these methods of their own accord, so it is a lovely gift to them if we can introduce such ideas at a young age.

USEFUL FURTHER READING

Gerhardt, S. (2015) *Why Love Matters: How Affection Shapes a Baby's Brain* (2nd edition). London and New York: Routledge.

Glouberman, D. (2003) *Life Choices, Life Changes: Develop Your Personal Vision with Imagework* (revised edition). London: Hodder & Stoughton.

IMPACT Essentials for Managing Stress

By doing the activities in this section you will be helping children to:

- think about different aspects of themselves, not just how they are dealing with any current difficulties
- identify their strengths and resources
- begin to explore how the ability to imagine can be a helpful resource
- explore the idea that feelings can change and that we can have some control over them
- understand that what we think affects how we feel and behave
- develop or consolidate their skills in focusing and attending.

1. Remember me

Wellbeing focus:

- ☑ Self-awareness
- ☑ Self-acceptance
- ☑ Self-reliance

Examples of personal skills learned or consolidated:

- ☑ Focusing attention
- ☑ Concentration
- ☑ Memory strategies
- ☑ Observation
- ☑ Taking turns
- ☑ Maintaining eye contact

Examples of general/social learning:

- ☑ Building self-respect and respect for others
- ☑ Appreciating diversity
- ☑ Understanding rules and how rules for games are made and can be changed

This is a good warm-up or group 'gelling' game, and can also lead into discussions about focusing and calming strategies.

How to play

Players sit in a circle. The first player says their own name. The second player says the first player's name and their own name, the third player says the first two players' names and their own name, and so on, around the group.

Adaptations

- Players can prompt each other if needed.
- Names are said in time to rhythmic clapping, to keep the momentum going.
- Alternate children in the circle take turns to say their own name and the name of the person sitting on their right. This second child claps twice but does not speak. If anyone claps when it is their turn to speak or speaks when it is their turn to clap, the whole process changes direction.
- The children introduce themselves and each other, making sure that they look at each person and gain eye contact with them as they say their names

(but be aware of any cultural differences in how comfortable children might feel with this adaptation when adults are included in the circle).

• In a large group, the facilitator sets a limit on how many names need to be remembered before a new player starts the next section of the group.

Talk about

Did anyone use any specific strategies to help them to remember names? What might help?

Is it harder or easier to remember names when you are concentrating on something else as well (such as clapping)? Does this apply to other tasks? Does it depend on what the task is?

In later games sessions this could be linked with trying to remember calming strategies. For example, 'If I'm trying to fix something and it's hard to do, it will be even harder if I get frustrated but easier if I remember to stay focused and calm.'

You may have chosen to shorten your name or use a nickname to reflect how you would like to be known. Why is it important to remember how other people would like to be known?

Do all games have rules? Do all groups need rules? Why/why not? What rules could be changed in this game? How are rules decided? What are the most important things to think about when we want to change the rules of a game?

What, if any, differences did you notice when you kept eye contact with a person while you said their name? When might it be difficult to keep eye contact with someone? When is it helpful? Do we generally look at someone else all the time when we are talking or do we look away sometimes?

EXPANSION ACTIVITY 1.1. STORY-TELLING

Tell a funny story about a teacher or group leader who keeps forgetting children's names. The more they worry about this, the more often they forget. What mischief do the children manage to get up to?! How do the children eventually help the teacher to remember names or to be less stressed? (See *Using Imagination, Mindful Play and Creative Thinking to Support Wellbeing and Resilience in Children* for ideas about constructing wellbeing stories.)

This could also be done as a story round with each player saying one sentence. The game coordinator moves the story on as needed: 'Then the children had a great idea about how to help!'

EXPANSION ACTIVITY 1.2. GETTING TO KNOW YOU/CHILL-OUT CARDS

Have a selection of cards on which there are single words or pictures of things that players might like to do or like to eat. For example, you might include chocolate, singing, cycling and so on. Try to include things that you think only one or two children might like. Distribute the cards around the group. Each player tries to get rid of their cards by asking the question 'Do you like...?' and handing over the appropriate card if the other person says 'Yes'. The aim is for each player to have as few cards as possible by the end of the time limit. This does, of course, require honesty in saying if you like something or not!

Collect all the cards together and discuss which ones are also suitable as 'chill-out' activities. Do any of the children already use any of these ideas to help them chill after a tiring or stressful event? Has this game inspired anyone to try something that they hadn't thought of before?

2. Mixing it up

Wellbeing focus:

- ☑ Self-awareness
- ☑ Self-acceptance
- ☑ Self-reliance

Examples of personal skills learned or consolidated:

- ☑ Tolerating frustration
- ☑ Listening
- ☑ Waiting
- ☑ Focusing attention

Examples of general/social learning:

- ☑ Awareness of others
- ☑ Exploring links between thoughts, feelings and actions

This is a variation of 'Simon says'.

How to play
The game coordinator demonstrates simple movements for the players to follow, such as 'stand on one leg', 'touch your ear', 'wave' and 'clap'. When the instruction is 'do this', players copy the movement. When the instruction is 'do that', no one is supposed to move. Anyone who moves by mistake stands still for the next two calls.

Adaptations

- Instead of standing still when mistakes are made, the players continue to join in but move to an inner circle.
- Play 'Simon says' while holding on to a parachute. Movements will be based on leg, head or whole body movements, for example 'stand on one leg', 'nod your head', 'shake your shoulders', 'shake your foot'. (As with all games involving the use of equipment, parachute games should be supervised by an adult at all times.)
- Vary the speed at which the calls are made.

Talk about

Is it easy or difficult to listen, think and do something all at the same time? What could make it easier? Talk about self-awareness and self-control. When we repeat something often enough, we begin not to notice what we are doing. Why might this be useful? When might it not be useful?

Sometimes our thoughts become automatic too. Automatic thoughts can sometimes be useful – they can save us thinking time. But if they are unhelpful thoughts then we can learn to recognize these and begin to take control of them.

33

3. Create that!

Wellbeing focus:

- ☑ Self-awareness
- ☑ Self-acceptance
- ☑ Self-reliance

Examples of personal skills learned or consolidated:

- ☑ Understanding and using non-verbal communication
- ☑ Concentration
- ☑ Observation
- ☑ Thinking independently

Examples of general/social learning:

- ☑ Adaptability
- ☑ Dramatic awareness

How to play

Players stand in a circle. The game coordinator mimes taking off a hat and passes this imaginary object to Player A. This player changes the hat into something else (such as a mixing bowl or a toy boat) and mimes using it or playing with it before passing it on to Player B. When the object has been all round the circle the game coordinator takes it back and wears it as a hat again. Players attempt to make the transformations from one object to another connect up in some way.

Adaptation

- Pass the same imaginary object around the circle for each player to use in a different way.

Talk about

In this game players used their imagination and creativity to come up with different ideas. In what ways do you use your imagination every day?

Think about having fun while experimenting and finding solutions for managing difficult situations. Sometimes there is no right or wrong way of doing things – there are just different ways!

EXPANSION ACTIVITY 3.1. WHAT ARE IMAGES?

(See *Using Imagination, Mindful Play and Creative Thinking to Support Wellbeing and Resilience in Children* for further guidelines on using imagery.)

Read activity sheet 3.1 together. This can be used as the basis for a group discussion. Allow each child the chance to contribute an idea that they feel came from their imagination. Compare and contrast these. Talk about the different types of images. For example, some will be like pictures, some will be sounds (such as imagining a conversation or a tune in your head) and some will be feeling or sensation images (like the feeling of velvet or mud). Sometimes we can have a feeling of sadness or anger or being happy just by imagining something.

EXPANSION ACTIVITY 3.2. IMAGINE A PLACE

Give the children the following instructions, leaving plenty of pauses to allow them time to explore the images:

> Close your eyes and settle yourself into a comfortable position in your chair. Slowly take three full breaths – in through your nose and out through your mouth... I'd like you to imagine that you are in your most favourite place... [Ask the children to give you a signal when they have found their favourite place to be.]
>
> Imagine all the details of this place. What can you see?... Notice the colours...shapes...sounds...and smells that are around you... Spend a few moments enjoying imagining that you are really there. What are you doing?... What are you thinking about when you are in this place?... When you are ready, open your eyes and draw or write about what you imagined. Tell someone else about your favourite place.

Talk about

How did you feel when you imagined your favourite place? Did you feel warm or cool? Did you feel relaxed or did you have tight muscles? What else did you notice?

Was it difficult or easy to remember somewhere familiar? Why was this? Do you think it is harder or easier to imagine somewhere made up or somewhere that you know well? Why do you think this? When you think about different places do you mostly remember what that place looks like? Do you remember the sounds that you can hear there? What about smells?

If you were at the seaside what would you be able to hear, smell, see and touch?

4. If I were an animal

Wellbeing focus:

- ☑ Self-awareness
- ☑ Self-acceptance
- ☑ Self-reliance

Examples of personal skills learned or consolidated:

- ☑ Concentration
- ☑ Understanding metaphors
- ☑ Observation
- ☑ Recognizing and understanding emotions

Examples of general/social learning:

- ☑ Building self-respect and respect for others
- ☑ Understanding diversity
- ☑ Developing sensitivity to other people's strengths and differences
- ☑ Exploring self-concept

This game requires a large space for the children to be able to move around. For the adapted version everyone will need a turn at directing others in how to be their animal, so it is best to do this version of the game with small groups or in pairs.

How to play

Take some time to think of some animal names and characteristics.

Each child thinks of an animal that somehow shows something about who they are. Divide the group into two. Half the group imagine becoming their chosen animal for a short while – moving around the room, greeting other animals and finding out their 'character'. The other half of the group sits and watches. Those who are watching can get up at any time and tap an animal on the shoulder to guess its identity. If the guess is correct that animal joins the observers. Keep going until all the animals have been guessed. The groups then swap over.

Adaptations

- The game coordinator chooses one of the animals from the above game. Everyone in the group tries to act like that animal for 30 seconds. The person who originally chose the animal (in the first game) can give 'directions'; for example, 'I'm a mountain lion and I move like this. I speak like this. I don't like...but I do like... When I meet other mountain lions I...'
- Ask the children to choose a completely different animal, perhaps one that has the opposite characteristic to the first one chosen. For example, if a child chose a noisy animal, they could try being a quiet one, fast/slow, big/small, etc.
- All the children go back to being their original animals and stand or sit in a circle to introduce themselves to the group and say one good thing about being this animal (for example, 'I'm a leopard and I can run very fast'). Finish by 'stepping out' of the chosen animals – invite the children to have a stretch and shake their arms and legs and to go back to being children again.

Talk about

What did it feel like to be the animal that you chose? How are you like that animal? Did you find out anything new about anyone else?

Do you think you are sometimes like the first animal and sometimes like the second one? How does that feel? We can have different levels of the same feeling or characteristic in different situations. For example, we could be energetic one minute and very sleepy the next; or happy and then suddenly sad; timid in one situation and very brave in another.

How did it feel to be like someone else (your chosen animal)? Was it easy or difficult? Are you ever like that yourself?

EXPANSION ACTIVITY 4.1. FINDING OUT A BIT MORE

This activity uses one of the basic formats of ImageWork: becoming the image in order to find out more about it. Instead of choosing an animal to reflect who they are, players choose an animal to reflect how they would like to be. Remind children to accept each other's images in a respectful way. (See Chapter 9, 'Image-Making', in the accompanying eBook *Using*

Imagination, Mindful Play and Creative Thinking to Support Wellbeing and Resilience in Children for further guidelines for using imagery.)

Read the following instructions aloud slowly, to give the children time to notice what is happening in their imagination. Ask for feedback as you go along: 'Would anyone like to tell me what animal they are?' or 'Who wants to tell us what they wish for this animal?' This will encourage a feeling of connection between group members and will help you to know what's happening. It also helps those who need more time to explore their images or who are having any difficulties getting an image in the first place. Invariably, the group will not all be working at the same pace. Move on when it feels right to do so. When you have finished, encourage the children to draw the animal that they chose.

If I were an animal

Close your eyes and take three full breaths, letting the air out slowly as you breathe out.

When you are ready, I'd like you to imagine that you could be any animal you wanted. What animal would you be?...

Now imagine that you *are* this animal... Step into being the animal and really feel what that is like... Do you make a sound? What sounds do you make?... Do you move?... If so, how do you move?... Where do you live?... What do you like doing?... What do you not like doing?... What is the best thing about being you?... Is there anything that is not so enjoyable?... What would you most like to be able to do?... What do you most wish for?... Now step out of being this animal and back to being you.

Give yourself a shake all over. Shake your legs...shake your arms...and your hands... When you are ready, open your eyes.

Talk about

As a group make a list of all the different characteristics of the chosen animals. What did each child particularly like about their chosen animal? Why was this? (Relate some of these to everyday experiences where appropriate. An admired characteristic might be 'fast' and you might be able to relate this to being physically fast or to being a quick thinker, but remember, you are not interpreting the images, just putting forward tentative links.)

How confident did you feel as your chosen animal?

Did anyone think of things that might not be so enjoyable about being their chosen animal? How does this relate to daily experiences? For example, a lion cub might be considered so brave that they are expected to face more scary situations than any other animal of the same age.

Which animal is your brother/sister/friend like? Why do you think that?

EXPANSION ACTIVITY 4.2. EVERYONE IS DIFFERENT

Complete activity sheet 4.2 together.

Talk about

What would life be like if each of us were exactly the same? Imagine what your family would be like. What about your class or your street or town or the world?! (Invite fantastical answers to this as well as more logical ones.)

What would be one good thing about everyone being the same? Think about 'sameness' in such things as looks, actions, likes and dislikes. What would not be good about all being the same? Why would that be difficult? What would happen then?

We each have different ways of managing difficult feelings, thoughts and situations. What works for a friend or someone in your family may not be exactly right for you, and what works for you may not be right for them. It's important for you to try things that we know will help most people and then you can find out which way is best for you.

EXPANSION ACTIVITY 4.3. SOMETHING IN COMMON?

Invite the children to draw a picture of someone they know well and who they think is similar to them in some way.

Talk about

Sometimes you can find ways that people are similar. For example, people can be alike in the way that they look, how they behave, where they live, what they like to do or to eat and what they don't like. Think of someone in your class or group who is like you in some way. What is their name? How is this person like you?

Do you know someone who is like you in lots of ways? What is their name? How are they like you? What is good about knowing people who have the same or similar interests as you? We are all unique, but we can have things in common with others as well.

Do you think everyone feels relaxed and calm all the time? Do you think your friend/brother/sister sometimes feels 'stressed out'? Why do you think this? How do people show that they are relaxed? How do they show that they are feeling energetic? How do they show that they are feeling tense? Do you think anyone else has the same or similar worries as you have?

41

5. Circle move

Wellbeing focus:

- ☑ Self-awareness
- ☑ Self-acceptance
- ☑ Self-reliance

Examples of personal skills learned or consolidated:

- ☑ Concentration
- ☑ Observation
- ☑ Pausing and re-focusing
- ☑ Waiting/taking turns
- ☑ Understanding and using non-verbal communication

Examples of general/social learning:

- ☑ Development of body awareness and positive body image
- ☑ Awareness of different types of worry and stress

How to play

Players sit in a circle. One person starts off a movement such as a shoulder shake. Each player copies this in turn until everyone is making the same movement. Then everyone stops in turn until the circle is still. The person sitting to the left of the first player then starts a different movement and sends this around the group in the same way. Do this as many times as feels comfortable, varying the speed.

Adaptations

- In larger groups the movement can be started simultaneously by every third or fifth child, so that players do not need to continue the movement for too long.
- Two players sitting on opposite sides of the circle start off two different movements at the same time and send them in the same direction or in opposite directions.
- Players 'throw' the movement to each other across the circle by gaining eye contact with another player.

- Lengthen the period of stillness between the end of one movement and the start of the next.
- Use postures, facial expressions and hand movements that indicate different feelings.

Talk about

How easy or difficult was it for you to keep focused on the movement? Why was this? What were you doing/thinking/feeling while you were waiting for your turn? What does 'being focused' mean? How might being focused help us to become calm when we are feeling a bit stressed?

EXPANSION ACTIVITY 5.1. DIFFERENT FEELINGS

The children make shadow puppets by tearing pieces of paper into the shape of a person. Tearing the paper means that they don't have to try and be accurate about the size and shape of the person. You could also use card and paper fasteners to make moveable legs and arms.

Each child thinks of three things that might make them feel stressed or worried. Talk about all the different feelings that we might have when we are feeling worried or nervous about something, such as 'butterflies', hot hands, fast breathing, feeling grumpy. Each child chooses which feeling they will write on their own shadow puppet. They then collaborate in pairs or threes to put on a short puppet play that depicts the feelings – for example, a grumpy puppet that has butterflies that won't settle down.

Talk about

Have you each come up with different *types* of stress? An example of an emotional stress would be difficulties within a friendship, while a physical trigger to stress might be continuous loud noise or being in a crowded room. Mental stress might be something like studying for a test.

What are the similarities and differences in the lists that you made?

Think about times when a reasonable amount of stress can be useful. Make a list or draw times when 'a bit of stress' has helped you to achieve something.

Talk about how different people might have different feelings for the same emotion and how many feelings might be the same for everyone.

Do you set yourself goals to work towards? What would you most like to achieve by the end of next week? Next month? Next term? How will you know when you've achieved it? How will other people know that you've achieved it?

Thinking and Feeling

By doing the activities in this section you will be helping children to:

- understand why our bodies might react to 'false alarms'
- recognize the signs of stress
- understand that the way we think about a situation can affect how stressed we feel.

6. Guess how!

Wellbeing focus:

- ☑ Self-awareness
- ☑ Self-acceptance
- ☑ Self-reliance

Examples of personal skills learned or consolidated:

- ☑ Cooperation
- ☑ Observation
- ☑ Problem-solving
- ☑ Understanding and using non-verbal communication
- ☑ Identifying emotions
- ☑ Understanding opposites

Examples of general/social learning:

- ☑ Development of body awareness and positive body image
- ☑ Understanding links between feedback from others and self-monitoring

How to play

Two players leave the room while everyone else decides what 'tense/stressed position' or 'calm position' they should take up on their return. For tense this might be something like 'sitting on the floor with fists clenched and eyes closed'. For calm, the children might choose something like 'sitting on the floor with their hands resting on their lap and smiling'. The two players return and try to work out how they should be sitting or standing according to how loudly or quietly the rest of the group are clapping. The closer they get to the target position, the louder everyone else claps.

Adaptations

- The two players who left the room return and 'arrange' two other players in pre-chosen positions.
- Compare stressed and angry. What are some of the similarities?

Talk about

Are there times when stress and anger can become confused? Has there ever been a time when you have acted in an angry way because you were feeling upset or worried?

Sometimes we get feedback from others about whether or not we're succeeding in a task or we're 'on the right track', but sometimes we have to rely on our own self-awareness. Talk about being realistic in self-awareness. How do you know when you are doing something well? How do you know when you are tense or when you are relaxed? How do you know when it would be helpful to you if you did something in a different way?

EXPANSION ACTIVITY 6.1. FIGURE IT OUT

The children draw three or four 'gingerbread' people on a large piece of paper, and label each one with a different emotion. They take turns to add details on each picture to show what happens to us physically when we experience these emotions.

Talk about

When you look at all the figures, can you see anything that any of them have in common? What are the main differences?

What happens to our bodies when we are in a stressful situation?

When might a feeling of nervousness be useful? What other feelings might cause similar sensations in your body? For example, a knotted stomach could be excitement, clenched fists could be linked with determination. How does your body feel different when you are happy? What about when you are confident? If you are anxious and you change the way your body feels (perhaps by smiling and relaxing your muscles), do you start to feel a different emotion?

Sometimes it's hard to know what emotion we are feeling or why we are feeling a bit 'churned up'. Our body can react with 'false alarms' – we are just thinking worry thoughts but the body thinks we are in danger. Our imagination can cause the same reactions even when the situation has passed or when we are thinking about what *might* happen. Understanding more about how the body works can help us to recognize early warning signs and take action to prevent the build-up of more stress.

7. Worry stories

Wellbeing focus:

- ☑ Self-awareness
- ☑ Self-acceptance
- ☑ Self-reliance

Examples of personal skills learned or consolidated:

- ☑ Cooperation
- ☑ Concentration
- ☑ Listening
- ☑ Planning
- ☑ Sequencing/story-telling

Example of general/social learning:

- ☑ Developing sensitivity to other people's strengths and differences

How to play

Make a group list of things that children might worry about at school or when playing with friends. Small groups of children are invited to make up a short story about 'The day the worries took over our school/town'. They practise this together, taking an equal share in the telling. The groups then take turns to tell their story to the whole group.

Adaptation

- Make up a worry poem together. Each player contributes one word at a time while the game coordinator writes the poem out so everyone can see it. You could have rules about the length of the poem or perhaps there are certain words that must be used (but only when they make sense within the sentence). Anyone who successfully uses one of these words gets a second go.

Talk about

Do you think everyone has worries? Do people worry about the same sorts of things? Are some worries useful? What happens when worries take up a lot of thinking time and aren't resolved? Who do you share worries with? What could you do with your worries? How are worries different to problems? (See the next activity, '8. Shapes'.)

EXPANSION ACTIVITY 7.1. WORRY TEAMS

Divide the children into 'worry' teams (see Chapter 14, 'Group Structures for Playing IMPACT Games', in the accompanying eBook *Using Imagination, Mindful Play and Creative Thinking to Support Wellbeing and Resilience in Children* for examples of non-competitive ways to choose teams). Each team is given a particular worry that is common to most children. They have a set time in which to come up with as many ideas as possible to deal with this worry. Give the groups a one-minute countdown when it is almost time to complete the task. Just before the end of the minute suggest that they add one more idea. Teams can then present their ideas or pick one that they all agree on and present that.

Talk about
Did the most useful ideas come at the start of this activity or near the end, or was there a mixture? What does this tell us about dealing with worries?

8. Shapes

Wellbeing focus:

- ☑ Self-awareness
- ☑ Self-acceptance
- ☑ Self-reliance

Examples of personal skills learned or consolidated:

- ☑ Concentration
- ☑ Observation
- ☑ Understanding metaphors
- ☑ Problem-solving

Examples of general/social learning:

- ☑ Flexibility of thought
- ☑ Dramatic awareness

Ask the children to think of three or four common problems that might need solving such as what to do if a friend is being bullied, or what to do if they don't understand what the teacher has asked them to do. Imagine if each of these problems was a different shape and texture – what would they look like? How would they feel? Perhaps one is spiky or sticky or smelly or maybe it is slimy? When the children have agreed a shape for each problem, the game can begin.

How to play

Players stand in a large circle. The game coordinator picks one of the imaginary problems from a box or hat in the centre of the circle. They carry this problem back to their place in the circle, holding it in a way that indicates its size and shape. They then pass the problem shape around the group. Can players guess which problem the game coordinator has chosen? How will each player show what shape and texture they think it is? Do these invisible problems make a noise? Do they move when you have them in your hands? Do they jump from one person to another? It is up to the game coordinator to keep a tight check on these problems so they don't run wild!

When every player has had the chance to hold the problem, the game coordinator takes it again. Now the players have the opportunity to change the problem in some way. They can make it much bigger or make it very tiny, they can 'play' with it, reshape it, fold it up, scrunch it up and throw it away. They can do this as a whole group or one at a time or in pairs. How inventive can they be? The game coordinator finishes the round by putting the problem back in the box or hat – unless, of course, it has disappeared!

Talk about

Some worries are about problems that can be solved. Some worries are about things that can't be solved, but these worries *can* be tamed! It's good to know which sort of worry you are thinking about.

(Encourage recognition of previous experiences of problem-solving. It is helpful if children recognize that each time they solve a problem, they are creating new possibilities for themselves.)

EXPANSION ACTIVITY 8.1. LET'S IMAGINE

This is an imagery activity that also encourages the idea that 'problems' can come in different sizes, that some are more like challenges than unsolvable problems, that creative thinking is a valuable tool and that recognizing a problem in the first place will help us to deal with it more successfully (see activity sheet 8.1).

EXPANSION ACTIVITY 8.2. PROBLEMS, OPPOSITES AND SOLUTIONS

A combination of Personal Construct Theory and ImageWork, this activity is in three parts (see activity sheets 8.2a, 8.2b and 8.2c), the aim is to help children to see that seeking the complete opposite of an identified problem, or simply avoiding a problem rather than solving it, is not always the best option. Sometimes a problem changes in nature, sometimes it shrinks, sometimes we change how we think about it and sometimes we have to walk away from it. Persistent problems often require an inspirational idea!

For ideas about how to use and extend this activity see the accompanying eBook *Using Imagination, Mindful Play and Creative Thinking to Support Wellbeing and Resilience in Children* (Chapter 17, 'Image-Making and Wellbeing Stories' and Chapter 18, 'Helping Children to Create Their Own Wellbeing Stories').

EXPANSION ACTIVITY 8.3. SOLVED IT!

It is always useful to remind children that when they are looking at new problems they can draw on past experience and current skills to get them started. There will always be something, however small, that they are already doing or already know about that will help them (see activity sheet 8.3).

EXPANSION ACTIVITY 8.4. STILL PUZZLED?

Activity sheet 8.4 has been added at this point because so many children are reluctant or even afraid to ask for help when they need it. They may feel that this is further evidence that they are failing and may therefore use other strategies, such as watching other children and following their lead, or perhaps waiting passively until someone *offers* help. Feeling that it is okay to ask someone to repeat an instruction or that it is okay to say 'I don't understand' is a big step for many children, particularly for those with low self-esteem. Talking about this in a very 'matter of fact' way can help them to feel that it is a natural part of the learning process rather than a failure.

EXPANSION ACTIVITY 8.5. MENTORING STORIES

Ask the children to think about books that they have read, or stories that they have been told, that contain a strong theme of problem-solving. In small groups or pairs, children retell these stories and discuss the strategies that were used by the different characters.

9. Imagine this: Feeling tense and feeling relaxed

Wellbeing focus:

- ☑ Self-awareness
- ☑ Self-acceptance
- ☑ Self-reliance

Examples of personal skills learned or consolidated:

- ☑ Focusing attention
- ☑ Concentration
- ☑ Monitoring physical sensations

Example of general/social learning:

- ☑ Development of body awareness and positive body image

Activity sheets 9a and 9b for this image activity can be used as a reminder for the children. I suggest that they are copied separately so that children can draw their images on the back of the sheet. The 'Magic mirror' template in Appendix C of the accompanying eBook would also be appropriate for use here.

How to play

Encourage the children to move into a different space when they 'step into' the image and step out of it again. This is so that they can physically remove themselves from feelings of tension. You might also want to start with a brief focusing activity (for example, '26. Getting ready for listening'). Otherwise use a simple 'settling' by focusing on three breaths as described here.

Begin with a very short description of tension or a reminder if you have already discussed this. For example:

Let's think about what our bodies feel like when we have different emotions.

Think of a time when you felt a bit upset or cross about something. I bet your body felt very stiff and perhaps you felt a bit churned up inside? Sometimes if we are very anxious or nervous about something it shows in our body too. Our muscles become tight. Maybe they begin to ache a little bit. We might feel 'knotted up' inside. This is called tension. This can feel very uncomfortable.

Then, when the children are ready, read the following slowly and calmly, giving them plenty of time to follow your instructions.

> When you are ready, close your eyes and take a full breath, letting the air out slowly as you breathe out... Do that two more times.
>
> If tension was an animal or a plant or anything else, what would it be?...
>
> Imagine something that somehow shows us what it's like to be tense...
>
> Imagine that you can become your image of tension... Step into being this plant or animal or object... What do you feel like when you are this image?
>
> What does your body feel like?... What is the worst thing about being this image?... Feel a frown growing from way down inside you... Feel it spreading all the way through you... Really notice what this is like...
>
> Now step out of being this image and back to being you... Give yourself a shake all over...shake your hands, shake your arms, shake your body, shake your legs! Let all that tension disappear...
>
> Draw or write about your image of tension. When you have finished, we'll do the next bit of imagining...
>
> When we are not tense our body feels more relaxed. If the feeling of relaxing was an animal, a plant or an object, what would it be?
>
> Close your eyes and take three full breaths, letting the air out slowly as you breathe out... Ask your imagination to come up with an image that somehow shows us what it's like to be relaxed... It could be an object, a plant or an animal... Whatever it is, just let the image appear...
>
> When you are ready, imagine that you can become your image of relaxation...
>
> Step into being this animal or plant or object and really feel what it's like...
>
> What does your body feel like?...
>
> Feel a smile grow from deep inside you... Feel it spreading all the way through you... Really notice what this is like...
>
> What is the best thing about being this image?
>
> Spend some time just being this image and enjoying the feelings... When you are ready, step out of this image and back to being you. Open your eyes slowly and have a stretch and a yawn!
>
> Draw or write about your feelings of being relaxed.

Talk about

If any children want to (they usually do!) then take time to share the images of being tense and being relaxed. Point out some similarities and differences between different children's pictures and also between the images produced by individual children.

> Laura (10), who at first told me she couldn't draw, produced a picture of herself lying on a sun lounger beneath a palm tree. Matthew (9) drew his cat curled up in front of the fire at home. Simon (9) drew a sunset.

How does your body feel when you are relaxed? Notice the difference between being very tense and feeling strong without feeling excessive tension. Spend time thinking of as many words as you can to describe what it's like to feel tense and relaxed.

Why is it important for our bodies to be relaxed sometimes? Is there such a thing as useful tension? When do we need to be tense? Are there times when you have tension in your body that doesn't need to be there?

For this activity players needed to use their imaginations. How could you use your imagination in the future to help you to feel calm?

IV

Exploring Strategies

By doing the activities in this section you will be helping children to:

- understand that they can change the way they cope with stress
- experiment with lots of different ways to deal with the effects of stress
- identify the strategies that work best for them.

10. Guess the voice

Wellbeing focus:

- ☑ Self-awareness
- ☑ Self-acceptance
- ☑ Self-reliance

Examples of personal skills learned or consolidated:

- ☑ Focusing attention
- ☑ Concentration
- ☑ Listening

Examples of general/social learning:

- ☑ Building persistence
- ☑ Building trust
- ☑ Extending awareness

How to play

Players stand or sit in a circle. Each player invents a unique vocal call, for example a combination of vowels with different intonation patterns or a hum or a whistle. The whole group listens to each call in turn as the players say their first name and then their chosen sound.

One person stands in the centre of the circle with a blindfold on. The game coordinator silently chooses someone to make their call. The person in the centre tries to name the caller. If they get it right they can have a second turn.

Each person has a maximum of two turns before the coordinator chooses another person to sit in the centre.

Finish with everyone back in the circle making their call at the same time and then stopping one by one around the circle until there is silence once more.

Adaptations

- Callers recite one line of a well-known song or a pre-chosen phrase that all the children are able to say/remember.
- Two people stand in the centre and can confer about the name of the caller.
- The person who was last in the centre can choose the next caller.

- Everyone changes seats before the caller is chosen.
- The players are split into pairs to practise their calls. One child from each pair then stands in the centre of the circle and is blindfolded. On a signal their partners make their chosen calls. The players who are blindfolded have to carefully move around the circle until they find their partner. The callers and their partners remain silent once they have found each other.

Talk about

What helps us to listen? Is it easier or harder for you to listen when you are blindfolded? Why is this? How do we recognize individual voices? What makes our voices sound different?

What words can we use to describe different voices? For example deep, gruff, loud, soft, like chocolate (keep these descriptions very general, rather than specific to individual children).

Does your voice change according to how you are feeling? How does it change?

How can listening and focusing skills help us when we are feeling a bit stressed?

EXPANSION ACTIVITY 10.1. MOOD MUSIC

Children take turns to be a conductor conducting the other children as they make their calls. See if they can moderate the volume of their calls. Can they produce different 'mood music' with their voices? How do they feel when they sing? How can singing help us to de-stress? Enjoy singing a well-known song together. Try one quiet song and one energetic song. What differences does everyone notice in the way they feel physically and mentally before, during and after singing these songs? (See '22. Musical drawing'.)

11. Body focus

Wellbeing focus:

- ☑ Self-awareness
- ☑ Self-acceptance
- ☑ Self-reliance

Examples of personal skills learned or consolidated:

- ☑ Focusing and shifting attention
- ☑ Concentration
- ☑ Monitoring physical sensations
- ☑ Self-calming
- ☑ Monitoring internal 'chatter'

Examples of general/social learning:

- ☑ Building trust
- ☑ Development of body awareness and positive body image

This activity is a simplified version of an exercise commonly taught as part of a mindful approach to life.[1]

Learning to relax the mind and body is a skill that needs to be practised regularly in order to reap its long-term benefits. Even the most tense-looking children eventually learn to let go of unnecessary muscle tension during relaxation sessions. You may have your own favourite method of relaxation to use, but it is worth experimenting with different types over a few sessions and asking for feedback from the children as to which one they found most helpful.

This body focus activity can be done lying down, for example on top of a parachute, or it can be done seated. Read each part slowly and calmly with plenty of pauses to allow the children time to follow your instructions.

The basic activity

When you are ready, let your eyes close gently and settle yourself into a comfortable position.

---

1   See, for example, Kabat-Zinn, J. (2020) *Full Catastrophe Living* (revised and updated edition). London: Piatkus.

Notice the feel of your body on the floor (or in the chair)...now gently move your attention to noticing your feet... Put all your attention on your feet and really notice what they feel like. Maybe they feel warm or cold; perhaps they are numb or itchy...tight or relaxed. Just notice whatever you can feel in your feet...

Now gently move your thoughts from your feet to the lower part of your legs. Let your thoughts leave your feet and just move very easily to your legs. Notice whatever feeling is there just at this moment... There are no right or wrong feelings... Whatever you can feel is okay... When your mind drifts off into other thoughts just gently bring it back to noticing your body.

Now move up to your knees...and then the top part of your legs, and notice whatever feelings are there... Now start to notice your tummy, feel what's happening when you breathe gently in and out...start to think about your shoulders... Notice all the feelings around your neck and your head...

Let your thoughts go gently to your back...all along the length of your back... Thinking about your arms now. Just notice whatever is there...and down the length of your arms into your hands... Notice all your fingers one by one. Whatever feeling is there, just notice it...

Now, keep noticing your body and start to listen to whatever sounds there are around you... Begin to move your hands and feet a little bit... When you feel ready, open your eyes and look around you... Lie or sit quietly for a short while before stretching and having a yawn.

Adaptations

Encourage the children to try out different brief focusing exercises using their imagination for different image modalities. Even if these images prove difficult to hold on to at first, continued practice will aid their ability to focus successfully and to bring the mind back from its natural wanderings (see *Using Imagination, Mindful Play and Creative Thinking to Support Wellbeing and Resilience in Children*). Children can practise extending the time for which they can keep their focus on the images.

The more simple the image, the more focused we need to be in order to keep it 'in mind'. Here are just a few examples.

- Visual:
  - Imagine the front door of your home.
  - Imagine a pen slowly writing your name on a piece of paper.

- Imagine different shapes of varying colours such as a purple triangle, a navy star and so on.

- Auditory:
  - Imagine the sound of a bell, a cat purring, rain on the window, a clock ticking.

- Tactile:
  - Imagine stroking a cat or a dog or a piece of velvet material.
  - Imagine holding a ball of rubber bands or an orange in your hand.

- Taste and smell:
  - Imagine eating a piece of soft fruit, chewing a toffee or drinking hot chocolate.
  - Imagine the smell of the sea, the smell of a bakery or the smell of a flower.

Talk about

What did you notice about your body?

How easy or difficult did you find this activity? Why do you think that?

How easy or difficult was it for you to focus on one image or one part of your body? Were some images easier to focus on than others?

What did you do or what did you say to yourself when you noticed that you were thinking about something else? How successful was this in helping you to focus back on your body/the image again?

EXPANSION ACTIVITY 11.1. RELAXATION

Often if we try to relax, we try too hard! In our efforts to relax we actually set up more tension. By observing what the body is doing there is a natural tendency simply to allow any areas of tension to relax and release. However, you can use the body focus with a specific emphasis on relaxation by adding a short introduction and completion.

Check that the room temperature feels comfortable. Have a blanket or duvet handy. Some children like the extra comfort of this if they are going to relax deeply. The next thing that you do after a relaxation should be very calm and slow.

As before, read each part very slowly and calmly with plenty of pauses to allow everyone time to follow your instructions. Start with:

> It's a really nice feeling to be able to relax your body...and it will help you to feel confident and more able to do things that are a bit difficult. When you are ready, let your eyes close gently and settle yourself into a comfortable position.

Read the body focus exercise to the children. End with:

> Now, instead of thinking of yourself in parts, feel your whole body relax. Just letting go...letting the floor (or chair) support you and just relaxing into it... As you breathe in, breathe in relaxation...and feel it spreading through every part of you...breathing in...and out...like waves on a seashore... Lie quietly for a few moments and enjoy the feeling of being relaxed... [Allow at least one or two minutes of quietness.]
>
> Keep noticing your body and start to listen to whatever sounds there are around you... Begin to move your hands and feet a little bit... When you feel ready, open your eyes and look around you... Lie or sit quietly for a short while before stretching and having a yawn...ready to slowly sit up...

Talk about

When you are feeling very stressed your brain is sending signals to your body to help you to run away or to fight. This can be really useful if you are in a dangerous situation, but it is not useful if you are just thinking about something horrible happening or you are getting worried about a test or about being late for school or not being able to find your favourite t-shirt. Your body gets full of 'stress' chemicals and this might make you feel angry or tired or very 'wobbly'.

If this happens then you can help your body to calm down again by doing exercise (like running or cycling or just going for a walk) or by doing a relaxation exercise and thinking about something nice. Then your brain sends different signals to the rest of your body so that 'feel good' chemicals are released. These will help you to feel more in control and more calm.

12. An alternative progressive relaxation

This activity is similar to the previous two but takes the focus on relaxation even further.

Find a really comfortable position to sit in, ready to let your whole body go loose... Let your body sink into the chair or cushion so that now you are as still as can be... Begin to think about your toes. Relax your toes and feel them getting warm and heavy... Let all the tightness just float away from your toe muscles so that they are not having to do any extra work... Now let go of any tightness in your legs. Put all your attention into your legs and let the muscles relax, release, let go... When your legs are relaxed begin to think about your tummy. Feel the muscles in your tummy go soft, relaxing and releasing any tightness that might have been there... Feel your hands and arms getting warm and heavy as they rest comfortably by your sides... Your fingers are very slightly curled but there is no tightness in them... Now think about your shoulders. It's easy to let our shoulders get tight when we're dashing about doing things all day, always in a rush. Gently raise your shoulders up towards your ears now and feel how the muscles have to work to keep them there... Then let go...and feel the difference... Notice how it felt when they were tight and how it feels when your shoulders are more relaxed...

Now let go even more than you thought you could... Think about your face. Feel a smile starting to come... Let the smile spread and spread until it reaches your eyes!... Now let go so that all the muscles on your face gently relax and your forehead feels a little wider and higher than it did before... If you haven't already shut your eyes, let your eyelids gently close now... Feel them become heavier and heavier so that you couldn't open them even if you tried...

Notice your breathing. Be very still as you feel the air going into your body when you breathe gently and quietly... Feel it as it slowly goes out again... In and out, like waves on the seashore... In...and...out... In...and...out... Now forget about your breathing and just feel yourself relaxing more and more... Imagine that there is a red light flowing up from the ground... It is flowing through your feet...through your legs...your body...your arms...your shoulders...and your head... It floats away through the top of your head and drifts upwards... Now your body is still relaxed but your mind is awake and ready to...[move on to the next activity].

13. Mindful breathing

Wellbeing focus:

☑ Self-awareness   ☑ Self-reliance
☑ Self-acceptance

Examples of personal skills learned or consolidated:

☑ Focusing attention   ☑ Self-calming
☑ Monitoring internal 'chatter'

Examples of general/social learning:

☑ Development of body awareness   ☑ Extending awareness
  and positive body image

I tend not to refer to 'deep' breaths as this can suggest to children that they need to put a lot of effort into taking a breath. 'Full' breaths can be explained as taking air right down into the base of the lungs.

The basic activity

Everyone sits in a circle. They place one hand lightly on their chest and the other hand just below their bottom ribs. Instruct everyone to take a full breath in through their nose while you count to four, gently pause for the count of two, and then breathe out gradually through their mouth while they notice what happens to their hands.

   Ideally, each child will have felt their stomach move downwards and outwards when they breathed in. There will have been only slight movement in their chest. Their shoulders will have hardly moved at all and their posture will have remained balanced. If a child raised their shoulders and expanded their chest or pulled in their stomach as they took a full breath, they were not breathing in a relaxed way. Once children have got the basic idea of relaxed breathing read the following instructions to them:

   Now gently close your eyes...and put all your attention into your breathing. Just noticing it without trying to change anything... Notice the feel of the air as you breathe in and the feel of the air as you breathe out... Keep noticing your breathing... When you have other thoughts just let them float through your mind and then go back to noticing your breathing again... We are going to carry on doing this for a little while...just sitting quietly, noticing how we breathe [do this for one minute].

Now you are ready to gradually open your eyes and...[move the children gently on to the next task].

Adaptations

- Gradually increase the length of time that the children sit like this. A good guide is to work towards one minute for each year of age.
- Ask the children to breathe in for the count of four. Then to gently hold the breath for the count of two and then breathe out for the count of four. They do this together with one other person. Now they both see if they can keep doing this while carrying out a simple task such as putting away some pencils together or walking around the room together.

Talk about

How do you feel when your breathing is calm? When might you need to have faster breathing? How easy or difficult was it for you to just notice your breathing? Why was that? Did you notice other thoughts come into your mind when you were sitting quietly? It would be very hard to stop these thoughts but it is good to notice when they come and then just let them go and put your attention back onto your breathing.

Note: Diaphragmatic breathing is very natural but may take a while to re-learn if a child's breathing pattern has changed over the years. Once children are able to direct their attention to the diaphragm they will notice themselves taking relaxing full breaths during the day and this will help them to feel calm. Suggest to children that they can also consciously take two or three relaxed breaths to help control any feelings of anxiety before these get too big (see '24. A brief 'calming' relaxation').

EXPANSION ACTIVITY 13.1. RELAXED BREATHING

Take some time to look at some pictures of the lungs and trachea (windpipe). Then look at activity sheet 13.1 together. It is useful to demystify the workings of the body so that children can realize that they have the ability to change their automatic reactions to stress and anxiety when these are not helpful to them.

The missing words are: lungs, oxygen, in, out, out, lungs, in, lungs.

EXPANSION ACTIVITY 13.2. AN IMAGE OF CALM BREATHING

Read activity sheet 13.2 to the children. Leave plenty of time at the end for them to draw their images and share them with each other. You might want to then give copies of this activity sheet to each child as a reminder of the activity or as an information sheet for parents or carers.

EXPANSION ACTIVITY 13.3. ENERGIZING BREATH

You will need to demonstrate this exercise for children as it can take quite a bit of practice!

Sit upright in a high-backed chair so that your body is well supported and relaxed.

Breathe naturally for a while, just feeling the rhythm of your breath.

After a few breaths, press your left nostril closed with your thumb and inhale through your right nostril. Keep the natural rhythm of your breath.

Release your thumb; close your right nostril with your forefinger and exhale through your left nostril.

Without changing fingers, inhale through your left nostril.

Change fingers. Exhale through the right nostril.

Inhale through the right and exhale through the left and so on. Repeat the whole sequence five times.

EXPANSION ACTIVITY 13.4. EXTENDING EXHALATION

As with Expansion activity 13.3 this also takes some practice.

> Sit erect and well supported; your chest and head in a straight line, shoulders slightly back, hands resting easily in your lap.
>
> Inhale slowly as you silently count to three (one...and...two...and...three). Remember to breathe from your diaphragm.
>
> Hold for the count of three.
>
> Exhale slowly through your nostrils, counting to six.
>
> Count to three again before inhaling.
>
> Continue this for about three minutes.

The reason for making the out-breath longer than the in-breath is that breathing in involves muscle contraction and the heart and metabolism speed up slightly. Breathing out involves relaxation of the muscles and the heart and metabolism slow down slightly. The duration of the out-breath can be slowly increased with practice. The important thing is to feel the rhythm rather than to try and increase the capacity too far.

14. Combining breath control and imagery

This works well if you imagine the seven colours of the rainbow as you breathe, starting with red close to the body and finishing with violet.

Ask the children to sit in a comfortable, upright position.

Imagine that you are the yolk inside an egg and that between the yolk and the egg are seven other layers. As you breathe in, imagine that you are breathing up the back of your body from the ankles to the top of your head. Pause for the count of three. Then as you breathe out, breathe down the front of your body, sweeping under your feet. Repeat this six more times, remembering the next time you breathe in to imagine that you have moved slightly further away from your body into the next level, so that when you reach the seventh in-breath you are sweeping a wide circle around your body. Really let go each time you breathe out, releasing the tension from your body. Take your time with this. There is no need to rush it.

Now the next time you breathe in, breathe up the right side of your body from the feet to the top of your head and down the left hand side of your body as you breathe out. Again, do this in a circular movement, sweeping under your feet and moving away from your body in a circle that gets bigger and bigger with each breath. Do this for seven breaths, remembering to pause after breathing in each time.

15. Mindful musical chairs

Wellbeing focus:

- ☑ Self-awareness
- ☑ Self-acceptance
- ☑ Self-reliance

Examples of personal skills learned or consolidated:

- ☑ Focusing attention
- ☑ Listening
- ☑ Cooperation

Examples of general/social learning:

- ☑ Development of body awareness and positive body image
- ☑ Spatial awareness
- ☑ Building trust
- ☑ Awareness of others
- ☑ Understanding empathy

The usual version of musical chairs consists of children dancing, walking or running around a line of chairs while the facilitator plays music. When the music stops everyone sits on a chair. There are always fewer chairs than there are children. This means that there will always be one or more players who won't have a chair to sit on and who will therefore be 'out'. When the music starts again another chair is taken away. This supposedly fun party game is often not remembered with any degree of fondness by adults! However, there are many ways in which this game can be adapted to be more mindful and to be cooperative rather than competitive.

How to play musical chairs mindfully

- Have enough chairs for only half the group. The children tiptoe around the chairs while music is played very quietly. When the music stops each child who is left standing partners with a child who is seated on one of the chairs. When the music starts again each pair of children walk around the chairs and attempt to breathe mindfully and in unison with each other.
- The children walk around the chairs in silence, focusing on their breathing or on the movements of their feet and the feel of their feet touching the

floor. After a few moments the game coordinator rings a bell or says quietly 'change over' and everyone moves in the opposite direction. The coordinator removes a chair. When the instruction to sit down is given, the person standing by the space left by the removed chair partners with the child on their right. This continues until all the children are in pairs. If there is an uneven number then the game coordinator pairs up with the last remaining player.

- Musical hoops – a number of large hoops are placed on the floor. The children move slowly around the room, weaving between the hoops while quiet music or bird song is played. When the music or bird song stops, the children step inside the nearest empty hoop. They stand very still in the hoops for 5–10 seconds, focusing on their breathing. Then the music starts again and one hoop is removed. By the time half the hoops have been removed in this way there will be two or three children in each hoop. See if they can breathe mindfully and in unison with each other.

EXPANSION ACTIVITY 15.1. NOTICING

Ask the children to notice times when they are aware of breathing calmly during the day or when they have consciously used mindful breathing to help themselves to feel calm and focused.

16. Melting ice sculpture

Wellbeing focus:

☑ Self-awareness   ☑ Self-reliance
☑ Self-acceptance

Examples of personal skills learned or consolidated:

☑ Monitoring physical sensations   ☑ Understanding opposites

Examples of general/social learning:

☑ Development of body awareness   ☑ Dramatic awareness
  and positive body image

How to play

The children spread out around the room so that each child has plenty of space in which to 'melt'. Players start by imagining that they are a newly built ice sculpture. They stand very still. Now they imagine the sun has come out and it is getting warmer and warmer. The sculpture starts to 'melt' until they are pools of melted ice on the floor. The children lie very still, letting all their muscles go floppy. Do this once more – building up into an ice sculpture and then melting. Then they are back to being children again. Ask them to stand up and shake their arms, hands and legs.

Adaptations

- Alternate between being a rag doll and a wooden or metal toy.
- Ask the children to work in pairs, with one child taking the role of sculptor and directing their partner how to stand or sit as a particular ice sculpture – perhaps a flamingo standing on one leg, or standing on tiptoe as a tree.
- The children melt very gradually. They see if they can tense one set of muscles and relax another at the same time. For example, they frown or clench their fist while letting their shoulders relax.

Talk about

How difficult or easy was it to hold your posture as an ice sculptor? Why was this?

How difficult or easy was it to 'melt' and to lie very still? Why was this?

What helped you to relax your muscles? Is it possible to have relaxed muscles when you are standing up? Why is this? Is it possible to relax some muscles and tense other muscles at the same time?

EXPANSION ACTIVITY 16.1. SELF-CALMING

I suggest that you use one of the shorter self-calming activities (from section V) as an expansion activity immediately after playing '16. Melting ice sculpture' and talk about the ways in which we can notice and release unwanted tension at any time without anyone even noticing that we have done this.

17. Switch over

Wellbeing focus:

- ☑ Self-awareness
- ☑ Self-acceptance
- ☑ Self-reliance

Examples of personal skills learned or consolidated:

- ☑ Concentration
- ☑ Observation
- ☑ Self-calming

Examples of general/social learning:

- ☑ Building trust
- ☑ Exploring links between thoughts, feelings and actions

Genuine laughter is thought to have anti-stress effects, activating the brain's emotion-regulating centres and causing the release of opioids, the natural brain chemicals that induce feelings of pleasure and wellbeing.[2] It has also been suggested that a good 'belly laugh' or 'a fit of the giggles' may have effects on our immune system. It might be that laughter induces a positive mood or that a sense of fun can help individuals to cope with stress more effectively. Whatever the science behind it, laughter is often a natural element of children's games, and having fun while learning is certainly a motivator for most of us.

Be aware of any cultural differences in the appropriateness of different levels of eye contact when playing this game.

How to play

Pairs sit facing each other. They choose who is A and who is B. They must keep eye contact and try to keep a straight face. The game coordinator waits until everyone is quiet and then says 'switch over', at which point Person A tries to make Person B laugh in any way they can without touching them. At any time the coordinator can say 'switch over' again and the players then swap roles.

---

2   Sunderland, M. (2006) *The Science of Parenting*. London: Dorling Kindersley. [There is now a second edition of this book, published in 2016.]

Adaptations

- Players lie down on the floor in a circle with heads nearly touching in the centre and feet facing towards the outside of the circle, their hands resting gently on their stomachs. The first person starts off by saying 'ha!', the second says 'ha ha!', the third says 'ha ha ha!', and so on, going as fast as possible until someone starts to laugh for real. Then everyone has to wait for silence before another player starts off a round of 'ho!'
- This can also be played with each person lying with their head on someone else's stomach. The movement involved in saying 'ha!' can cause laughter before the round gets very far at all!

Talk about

How easy or difficult was it for you to keep eye contact? Why was this?

Was it easy or difficult to stop yourself from laughing? Why was this?

How do you feel when you have had a 'fit of the giggles'? Talk about the difference between laughing *at* someone and laughing *with* someone. Sometimes laughing can help us to feel more relaxed. When might this be appropriate? When would it not be appropriate?

Have you ever felt upset or angry about something that you could laugh about later?

What makes you laugh? Laughter can have very different qualities and can therefore cause us to feel quite differently too.

Is it possible to make yourself laugh or smile just by thinking about something funny?

EXPANSION ACTIVITY 17.1. RESEARCH AND SHARE

Set the children the task of finding out some things that make friends and family laugh. Are there any similarities? Does anyone have a funny story to tell?

18. Image journeys

Wellbeing focus:

- ☑ Self-awareness
- ☑ Self-acceptance
- ☑ Self-reliance

This is a shorter version of '12. An alternative progressive relaxation' coupled with a guided visualization in which the children are invited to find an 'image' which will represent resilience. It will be helpful if the children have already played '3. Create that!' and have done 'Expansion activity 3.1. What are images?' in section II of this book. For further guidelines on using imagery with children please see Chapters 8 and 9 in *Using Imagination, Mindful Play and Creative Thinking to Support Wellbeing and Resilience in Children*. There is also a similar activity in *Helping Children to Manage Transitions* ('9. The resilience tree').

As part of this imagery children first discuss the meaning of resilience and the concept of resources for resilience. They then think of a name for something that might represent resilience (such as 'helpsme'). This will be used to name an object that they find on an imaginary walk. Once they have agreed a name, invite the children to sit quietly on their chairs or on the floor or on top of a parachute ready to stretch their imagination. I suggest that you join the children in this imagery so that you can get a feel for the timing of the questions and when it might feel right to move on. Read each part slowly and calmly with plenty of pauses to allow the children time to follow your instructions.

The basic activity

Find a comfortable position, ready to let your whole body go loose... Let your body sink into the chair (or floor) so that now you are as still as can be... Begin to think about your toes. Relax your toes and feel them getting warm and heavy... Slowly move your attention into your legs and let the muscles of your legs relax... When your legs are relaxed begin to think about your tummy. Feel the muscles in your tummy become soft and relaxed... Feel your hands and arms getting warm and heavy as they rest comfortably by your sides...

Think about your face. Feel a smile starting to come... Let the smile spread and spread until it reaches your eyes... Now let go so that all the muscles on your face gently relax... When you are ready allow your eyes to close... Let's imagine that we are all going on a short walk together... Imagine that we are standing on a path that leads us through the countryside... Notice your feet on the path... Notice what clothes you are wearing... What can you hear around you? What can you see? As we begin to walk along the path each of you will find something special that will be your (chosen name for resilience). It might be a stone, a leaf, a shell – something small that you can hold in your hand. Or it might be something big like a tree or an animal. Look around you as you walk along the path. When you have found something raise your finger (give me a 'thumbs up') so that I know. Would anyone like to tell us what they have found? Look closely at your (name for resilience). Look at all the details of its shape and colour... What does it feel like to touch? Does it make a sound? If so, what sound does it make? Does it have a smell? Really look and look and look – as if you are an artist and you want to know how to draw it... If this image of (resilience) could talk, what would it say to you? Does it have any advice for you? What do you want to say to the image? When you are ready thank your image and let it fade from your imagination. Now we are all going to walk back along the path... Here we are... Just where we started... Can you remember what your (name for resilience) said to you? Now gently bring yourself back to the room... When you are ready open your eyes... Give yourself a bit of a stretch and a yawn...(then slowly roll over onto your side and sit up).

Adaptation

- Instead of following a particular visualization, invite the children to imagine a special place where they like to be and to find their image of resilience in this place.
- Once the children are relaxed, tell a short wellbeing story about resilience (see Chapters 17 and 18 in *Using Imagination, Mindful Play and Creative Thinking to Support Wellbeing and Resilience in Children*).

Talk about

Briefly remind the children about internal and external resources for resilience. Did the images of resilience have any advice for any of the children? Make a list of different ways that we can relax our bodies and our minds. (Encourage the children to think about emotional 'busyness' as well as physical 'busyness' and how physical activity can be one way to relax the mind.)

EXPANSION ACTIVITY 18.1. PASS IT ON

Ask the children to teach a game, relaxation or self-calming activity to another child or to a member of their family. This works well if children from one class can teach another class, or if children work in pairs to practise a particular way of self-calming that they have each enjoyed doing so far.

19. Puppets

Wellbeing focus:

☑ Self-awareness   ☑ Self-reliance
☑ Self-acceptance

Examples of personal skills learned or consolidated:

☑ Cooperation   ☑ Observation
☑ Concentration   ☑ Monitoring physical sensations

Examples of general/social learning:

☑ Building trust   ☑ Dramatic awareness
☑ Understanding empathy

How to play

Players pretend to be puppets. They start in a standing position with their feet firmly on the ground, their arms stretched upwards and fingers spread out as though they are being held up by strings. They imagine that the strings are very slowly being loosened so that their body starts to drop down. Start with just the fingers, then hands, arms, head and upper body, finally bending slightly at the knees. The same movements are then performed in reverse until all players are standing upright again with arms stretched as high as they can. Do this several times at varying speeds. End with a shake to relax arms and legs again.

Adaptations

- Players make puppet movements in time to different types and speeds of music.
- In pairs, the players take turns at being the puppet and the puppeteer. Without touching the puppet the puppeteer pretends to pull strings to get different parts of the puppet to move in different directions and at different speeds. This works well if the puppet is lying down to start with and the

puppeteer has to work out which strings to pull in order to get the puppet to stand up.

Talk about

What aspects of movement can you control (speed, direction)? Think about the complicated sequence of movements needed to stand up or sit down. How do we learn how to do this?

What does it feel like to have a relaxed body? How does that compare to being tense?

When are you most relaxed? What sorts of things help you to feel relaxed? What might make you feel tense? Can you tell when your muscles are relaxed and when they are tense? Do you ever think about your shoulders, your back, the backs of your knees?!

How did the puppet and the puppeteer cooperate? What did you each need to do? How easy or difficult was this? Which role did you enjoy the most?

Is it possible to control our own thinking? When might it be easy to do this? When might it be difficult? (See the previous activities on worries and problems in section III.)

EXPANSION ACTIVITY 19.1. STORY-TELLING

Make up a story or puppet play about a shy animal who learns to be more relaxed with friends or a bird who copes with a stressful situation and so on. There are some ideas for constructing puppet plays and stories in *Using Imagination, Mindful Play and Creative Thinking to Support Wellbeing and Resilience in Children*. You might also have some favourites of your own that you could adapt. Children could then be the puppeteers and act out the story with ready-made puppets or some they have made for themselves (again, there are lots of ideas for these in *Using Imagination, Mindful Play and Creative Thinking to Support Wellbeing and Resilience in Children*). Choosing the type of puppet and how flexible or relaxed they can be is a useful part of the process.

20. Green space focusing

Wellbeing focus:

☑ Self-awareness   ☑ Self-reliance
☑ Self-acceptance

Examples of personal skills learned or consolidated:

☑ Focusing attention   ☑ Observation
☑ Pausing and re-focusing   ☑ Listening

Example of general/social learning:

☑ Exploring links between
   thoughts, feelings and actions

The children will need to do '13. Mindful breathing' before doing this so that they are not forcing their breath. For the final part of this activity each child will need their own hoop or circle of string (or one circle to share with one or two other children if you have a large group).

The basic activity
Find a shady 'green' space outside. Under a tree would be ideal. Read the following instructions with plenty of pauses to allow time for the children to absorb the information.

> For this activity we need to start with our backs as straight as possible (the best position is to be seated cross-legged on the ground) so that we are perfectly balanced and relaxed. Relax your shoulders. Put one hand on your tummy and feel what happens when you breathe. As you gently take a breath in, feel the air go all the way down into your lungs. Because your lungs need room to fill up with air, your tummy will come outwards, your shoulders will hardly move at all. When you breathe out, your tummy will move inwards. Now forget about your breathing for a while. Just let the air go in and out without thinking about it. Gently close your eyes and put all your attention into listening.
>
> What can you hear? Turn your head just a little bit to your right. What

can you hear now? Cup your hands over your ears so that you can hear what is behind you.

Now cup your hands over your ears so that you can hear what is in front of you.

Now rest your hands gently in your lap and listen some more.

Take a few moments for the children to talk about what they can hear.

When you are ready, open your eyes and look down at the ground. What can you see? Now look up and all around you. Can you see anything that you hadn't noticed when we first sat down here?

Now you are going to take your hoop (or string) and find a space to look even closer at the ground. Lie on the ground and look really closely at everything that is inside the hoop. What can you see?

Take a few minutes for the children to talk about all the things that they can see. Then come back to sitting together in one large circle.

Talk about

How did you feel when you had finished this activity? Did you see or hear anything that surprised you?

Do you ever notice yourself looking at something or listening to something while thinking about something completely different?

Can you listen, look and 'do' all at the same time? What might make this easier? What might make it harder?

EXPANSION ACTIVITY 20.1. GREEN SPACE LISTENING

Listen to three different bird songs and try to locate the birds. Or use a birdsong website to listen to three different calls made by one bird (including an alarm call).

Talk about

How are the calls different from each other? What words can be used to describe the differences? Do you think that animals and birds ever get stressed? What sorts of things might be stressful for them? Do people ever get stressed by similar things? Imagine being an animal or a bird. As this animal or bird, how would you relax or calm yourself?

Do you ever do things that help you to get ready to concentrate? What helps? Why does this help? Do you concentrate better when you are tense or when you are relaxed? (Or does it depend on what you are doing?) Why do you think this?

21. Circle massage

Wellbeing focus:

☑ Self-awareness   ☑ Self-reliance

☑ Self-acceptance

Examples of personal skills learned or consolidated:

☑ Cooperation   ☑ Taking turns

☑ Concentration   ☑ Monitoring physical sensations

Examples of general/social learning:

☑ Developing self-respect and respect for others   ☑ Understanding empathy

Positive touch, such as this type of massage (performed by children on each other), can have a calming and relaxing effect. Incorporating a regular period of massage into a child's daily routine can help to increase concentration levels, decrease levels of agitation and aggression and help children to learn skills of empathy and tolerance (see 'Positive touch' in section I).

The basic activity

Players sit in a circle with their backs to each other. Each player asks the person in front of them for permission to give them a massage. Players silently massage each other's back, neck and shoulders for two minutes. When the time is up everyone thanks the person who gave them a massage.

Adaptations

- Players offer each other a back and shoulder massage in pairs. This helps the giver and receiver to really concentrate on what is happening. The receiver can ask their partner to alter the massage, for example by going more gently or more slowly.
- Players take turns to close their eyes while their partner slowly draws a shape (circle, square, triangle) or writes a word on their palm with one

finger. The person with their eyes closed has to guess the shape or word. They can ask for up to three repetitions if it is hard to guess. If they get it right they swap places.

- In pairs, players take turns to 'drum' on each other's back (very gently) with their fingertips. They finish by laying their palms on their partner's back and resting there quietly for 30 seconds.
- Players give themselves an imaginary hair wash, using fingertips to massage their own heads.
- One player sits facing away from the group. Everyone takes turns to spell out their name in large letters on this person's back. If the first player guesses the name correctly the two swap places.

Talk about

How do you feel after this?

How does this help us with other activities?

Are you aware of sensations all the time? For example, do you notice your sleeves against your arms all day?

Why is it important to be able to change the focus of our attention from one sensation to another or from one task or object to another? Is it possible to pay attention to two different senses or two different tasks at once?

22. Musical drawing

Wellbeing focus:

- ☑ Self-awareness
- ☑ Self-acceptance
- ☑ Self-reliance

Examples of personal skills learned or consolidated:

- ☑ Focusing attention
- ☑ Concentration
- ☑ Listening

Example of general/social learning:

- ☑ Exploring links between thoughts, feelings and actions

The basic activity

The game coordinator plays a variety of music and the group draws whatever comes to mind while listening to the different rhythms and moods.

Adaptation

- The children bring in their own selections of music and talk about how they feel when they listen to them.

Talk about

Does listening to music affect how you are feeling? Is there a piece of music that always makes you feel sad or always helps you feel happy? Why do you think this is?

Are other members of the group affected in the same way by the same piece of music? Why do you think this is? Are you able to imagine a piece of music without actually hearing it?

How can you use the images that you drew to help you to feel calm, happy, in control etc. in the future? Is there some music that you could listen to that would help you to feel calm when you've had a stressful day?

EXPANSION ACTIVITY 22.1. TAKING CARE OF MYSELF EVERY DAY

Invite the children to contribute to a list of 'Ways to look after myself' (see activity sheet 22.1). This might include such things as going for a walk, having a 'quiet time', 'playing with my dog/cat', 'having a hug', etc. Try and get at least 20 items on the list. Each child can then decide on up to three things that they will do when they are feeling worried, fed up or tired during the next week. Be specific. For example, 'When I notice signs of stress...' or 'When I notice myself getting up tight...' 'I will go for a 10-minute walk'; 'relax on my bed'; 'take some time for myself'; 'play with the dog'; 'talk to a friend'...

Talk about

How is 'taking care' when you are doing schoolwork different to 'taking care' of yourself? (See 'Talk about' for activity '18. Image journeys'.)

Self-Calming

This section contains several shorter activities that children can use as 'emergency' de-stressors or in preparation for an event before they begin to feel stressed.

23. Fidget flop

This can be done at any time as a brief way to release tension and is useful prior to an activity that requires a lot of concentration. Read the instructions slowly, allowing as much time as feels comfortable for children to 'play' with the movements.

The basic activity

Imagine that your fingers are all animals or people and they're having a pretend play-fight. Make them play at fighting each other. Get them tangled up and then untangle them again... Now let them slowly stop...and then make them float instead. Let your fingers float around each other without touching...and now gently stroke your fingers across each other... Now have them fight each other again. They're moving faster and faster... Gradually they slow down... Can you feel them tingling? Let your fingers gently float around each other again... Now let your hands flop down as though they've gone to sleep.

Adaptation

- The children imagine that they are holding a soft ball in both hands. They can squeeze the ball tightly and then let it expand again, or squeeze and mould an imaginary ball of clay.

24. A brief 'calming' relaxation

For this quick relaxation to be effective it is best if the children have already experienced more detailed methods, particularly '13. Mindful breathing'.

When you're comfortable, close your eyes gently. Just let them close, as though you were looking down at your cheeks, and let your eyelids become so heavy that you couldn't open them even if you tried... Your eyes feel relaxed now, and that nice relaxed feeling slowly moves down over your face...your arms...your body...your legs...and your feet... Every part of you relaxing, feeling warm and more and more relaxed.

Now take a full breath three times. As you breathe in, imagine that you are breathing in calmness and relaxation, and as you breathe out, let all the tightness in your body float away... Breathing in relaxation... Breathing out tightness... Breathing in relaxation... Breathing out all your worries...and once more... Breathing in relaxation... Breathing out tightness...

Then coming up from the ground, imagine an orange light that travels through your feet...your legs...your body, your hands and arms...your shoulders, your neck and your head...and out through the top of your head, floating away like clouds on a summer day. Now you feel very relaxed but your mind is wide awake and ready to [move on to the next activity].

25. Be calm

Explain to the children that as soon as they notice themselves getting tense or worried they can say to themselves 'Be calm'.

They then focus on their hands as they breathe in (this doesn't have to be a big breath, just normal breathing) and, as they breathe out very slowly, allow their hands to relax. On the next breath they focus on their shoulders, and as they breathe out they allow their shoulders to relax. Finally they focus on their jaw and allow their jaw to relax as they slowly breathe out. After two or three more calm breaths they continue with whatever they were doing.

26. Getting ready for listening

The following provides a brief focusing activity.

> It's nice to rest quietly sometimes and to listen with the whole of our body, not just our ears. Let's see where our listening takes us today. Gently close your eyes and feel yourself relaxing all over so that every bit of you feels heavy and loose. When you breathe in you can feel a lovely warmth filling up your body. Each time you breathe out you are breathing away all the tightness in your muscles that you don't need when you are just listening. Feel the air as it very slowly goes in and out of you... Imagine that there is a yellow light that is coming up from beneath your feet. It moves through your feet...your legs...your body...your arms...your shoulders...and your head...and it goes through the top of your head and floats away...so now you feel very relaxed but still wide awake and able to listen with every little part of you.

Adaptation

- Encourage the children to choose their own colour for relaxation.

Talk about

Instead of a colour, what else could you imagine that would help you to feel relaxed but 'alert' and ready to listen? Do you always need to feel relaxed in order to listen? Why do you think this?

Wind Downs and Completions

The activities in this section can be used at the end of a single session of IMPACT activities or when a group is coming to an end. Wind-down activities teach simple strategies for 'letting go' of any leftover feelings that may have manifested during earlier games and discussions, or that may arise in the future. They do not involve any further discussion or expansion activities.

27. Fill your suitcase (or backpack)

Wellbeing focus:

☑ Self-awareness   ☑ Self-reliance

☑ Self-acceptance

Examples of personal skills learned or consolidated:

☑ Concentration   ☑ Understanding metaphors

☑ Observation

Example of general/social learning:

☑ Understanding empathy

How to play

Players imagine that they each have a suitcase (or backpack) that they are going to take away with them to remind them of all that they have learned and tried out. They can put anything they like in it – a skill that they have developed, a new game that they have learned, something important that someone said to them... What will they put in their suitcase (or backpack) today? Go around the circle or ask for volunteers to say what they will pack.

Adaptation

- Ask a child to take an imaginary gift from a treasure chest in the centre of the circle and to present it to the person sitting next to them. They tell them what the gift is and why they are giving it to them.

Talk about

How will you remind yourself of your achievements? Sometimes we carry heavy suitcases of worries and troubles with us everywhere we go. Try experimenting with carrying this suitcase (or backpack) for a while instead!

28. Parachute wind downs

If you have been using a parachute for some of the games, try the following:

- Invite all the children to lie still under the parachute while game coordinators gently float it up and down over the top of them.
- The children sit around the outside edge of the parachute and pass a smile or a hand squeeze around the circle.
- Invite the children to lie quietly on top of the parachute, listening to some gentle music or a short story.

29. Closing circles

At the end of each IMPACT session bring everyone back together again in a circle and finish with each person having the chance to say one brief thing before they leave. For example:

I feel…

Today I found out that…

Today I felt..

I have noticed that…

I feel really good about…

Adaptation

- The children do a round of 'I'm brilliant at…' or 'I feel really good about…', expressing the appropriate emotion strongly through body language and facial expression for others to reflect back.

VII

Activity Sheets

The activity sheets in this section can be adapted for discussion or used as a basis for devising more complex activity sheets for older children.

Where possible, I suggest that you encourage children to draw rather than to write, and to work together rather than to sit quietly completing activity sheets on their own. This sharing and talking will not only help to foster collaborative, mutually respectful relationships, it also offers an opportunity for each child to enrich their understanding of the benefits of using imagery, being mindful and thinking creatively.

ACTIVITY SHEET 3.1. WHAT ARE IMAGES?

Have you ever made up a story in your head? Imagined that you saw something that wasn't really there? Heard a noise and imagined that it was something scary? Have you ever remembered the taste or feel of something that isn't actually in front of you? Do you ever imagine that you are somewhere else or doing something different?

These are all images and they come from your *imagination*.

We all have the power of imagination and we can all use our imagination to help ourselves to sort out problems, feel good, cope with troubles when they come along and to help us to do the things that we want to do.

Have a go! If 'happy' was an animal, a plant or an object, what would it be? Draw your image of 'happy' here.

Now you're giving your imagination a good workout!

ACTIVITY SHEET 4.2. EVERYONE IS DIFFERENT

Think about two different people in your family or two of your friends.
Make a list of or draw some of the ways in which these two people are different from each other.

ACTIVITY SHEET 8.1. LET'S IMAGINE

Imagine if problems were animals or plants or anything at all that could be drawn. What would they be? Fill this page up with drawings that somehow show us what little problems and medium-sized problems and really big problems are like.

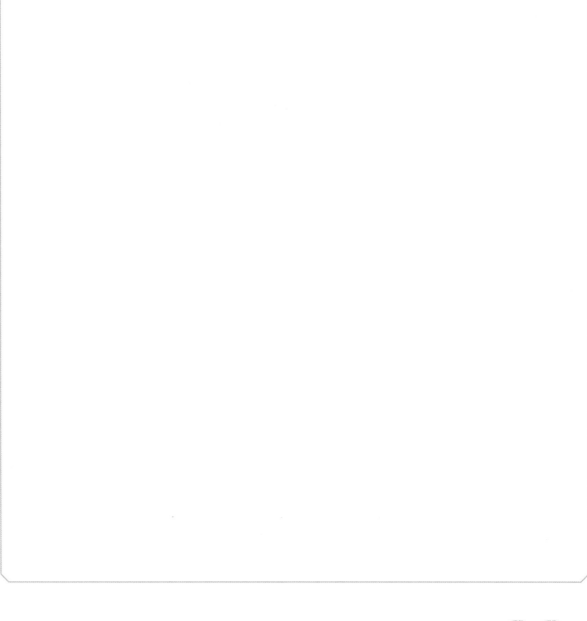

ACTIVITY SHEET 8.2A. PROBLEM TALK

Choose one of your 'problem' pictures and give it a name – for example 'friend problem' or 'homework problem' or 'maths problem'. If you could talk to your image problem what would you want to say to it? What does it say back to you? Imagine yourself having a conversation with it. Do you want to ask it to do anything? When you are ready, draw or write about what happened.

ACTIVITY SHEET 8.2B. OPPOSITES

Now imagine the opposite of the problem you chose. What does this look like? Imagine its colour, how it feels to touch, its size and weight. Draw the opposite of the problem image here.

ACTIVITY SHEET 8.2C. SOLUTIONS

Now draw a third picture. Fill the whole page with a picture that somehow shows us a solution (an answer) to the problem.

ACTIVITY SHEET 8.3. SOLVED IT!

Think of a time when you solved a problem on your own. Draw or write about it here.

ACTIVITY SHEET 8.4. STILL PUZZLED?

Sometimes we meet problems that we just don't understand at all. It's as if the problem came from another planet!

Draw or write about what you could do if you come across something that you don't understand or that you need help with.

If I don't understand something I could

....

....

....

....

ACTIVITY SHEET 9A. FEELING TENSE

Think of a time when you felt a bit upset or cross about something. I bet your body felt very stiff and perhaps you felt a bit churned up inside? This is called *tension*.

If tension was an animal or a plant or anything else, what would it be?...

Close your eyes and imagine something that somehow shows us what it's like to be tense...

Imagine that you can become your image of tension... Step into being this plant or animal or object... What do you feel like when you are this image?

What does your body feel like?... What is the worst thing about being this image?... Feel a frown growing from deep inside you... Feel it spreading all the way through you... Really notice what this is like...

Now step out of being this image and back to being you... Give yourself a shake all over...shake your hands, shake your arms, shake your body, shake your legs! Let all that tension disappear...

ACTIVITY SHEET 9B. FEELING RELAXED

When we are not tense our body feels more *relaxed*.

If the feeling of relaxing was an animal, a plant or an object, what would it be?

Close your eyes and take three full breaths, letting the air out slowly as you breathe out... Ask your imagination to come up with an image that somehow shows us what it's like to be relaxed... It could be an object, a plant or an animal... Whatever it is, just let the image appear...

When you are ready, imagine that you can become your image of relaxation...

Step into being this animal or plant or object and really feel what it's like...

What does your body feel like?...

Feel a smile grow from deep inside you... Feel it spreading all the way through you... Really notice what this is like...

What is the best thing about being this image?...

Spend some time just being this image and enjoying the feelings... When you are ready, step out of this image and back to being you. Open your eyes slowly and have a stretch and a yawn!

ACTIVITY SHEET 13.1. RELAXED BREATHING

Imagine that your lungs are like balloons. They can get bigger when you fill them with air and then they get smaller again when you let some of the air out.

Sit upright in a chair and put one hand on your stomach. Feel what happens to your stomach when you breathe in and out.

When you think you know what relaxed breathing feels like, see if you can fill in the missing words below.

When I breathe, the air goes in and out of my l _ _ _ _.

I breathe in air that is full of o _ _ _ _ _ and this helps to keep my body working well.

When I am relaxed and breathing easily my stomach goes _ _ and _ _ _.

When I breathe in my stomach moves _ _ _ because my _ _ _ _ _ are filling up with air.

When I breathe out my stomach goes _ _ because some of the air is going out of my _ _ _ _ _.

ACTIVITY SHEET 13.2. AN IMAGE OF CALM BREATHING

Calm breathing helps you to feel well and relaxed. It is especially helpful to have calm breathing if you have to do something that you are a bit worried about.

Doing some calm breathing before or after (or even *during*) a difficult time helps your body to relax once more. See if you can work your imagination again.

Close your eyes and ask your imagination to come up with an image that somehow shows us what it's like to have calm breathing. It could be an image of an animal, a plant or an object. Whatever it is, just let it come into your mind.

Now look at the image very closely. Let your imagination look at it from the sides, from the back, from underneath and from the top (as though you are looking down at it). Take your time exploring the image of calm breathing.

Now see if you can *become* your image and really feel what it is like to be the image of calm breathing. Just imagine yourself stepping into your image and becoming it. Take a full breath and let it go on a sigh. Now ask yourself 'what is the best thing about being this image?'... What can you do as this image?... If you can move, how do you move?... How do you feel now?...

Remember that whenever you are feeling a bit tense or worried, thinking of this image will help you to relax a little bit and to have the calm breathing that you need...

When you are ready, step back into being you. Thank your imagination for showing this to you... Let the image fade away... Gradually feel yourself coming back to the room...and open your eyes...so you are ready to draw or write about your image of calm breathing.

Now you are really giving your imagination a good work out!

ACTIVITY SHEET 22.1. TAKING CARE OF MYSELF EVERY DAY

Imagine that you've had a very busy day at school and you feel quite tired.

Think of all the things that you could do now to help yourself to feel relaxed and refreshed. Draw or write about them here.

Ask at least three other people what they like doing to help themselves to relax. Write or draw their answers here.